C, + H,

59 - 6733

1-13-60

British Policy in Changing Africa

NUMBER ONE *Dahomean Narrative* by Melville J. and Frances S. Herskovits

NORTHWESTERN UNIVERSITY African Studies

Number Two

BRITISH POLICY IN
Changing Africa

Sir Andrew Cohen

Northwestern University Press

Evanston

This volume has been published with the aid of grants to the Program of African Studies by the Carnegie Corporation of New York and the Ford Foundation. Neither of these, however, is responsible for any of the opinions expressed in this work.

Foreword

There is perhaps no one who can speak with greater authority on the subject of changing British policy in Africa than Sir Andrew Cohen. As head of the Africa Division of the Colonial Office, he was responsible for many of the measures that set the pattern of flexibility which has marked British post-war activity in the continent, and which has brought into being one new state, Ghana, and will within a short time grant independence to Nigeria. As Governor of Uganda, he was charged with implementing in the field many of the policies he promulgated, a task which he approached with the broad human sympathy for which he is everywhere known.

This book gives ample evidence of his point of view, couched in terms of realism that comes from a profound understanding of not only the aspirations of subject peoples, but also of some of the things they need in order to make good their freedom in the world of today. "A sense of responsibility," he tells us in one place, "can only be acquired by exercising responsibility." Again, he reads us the same lesson in more homely terms, when he points out that "you cannot learn to play the violin except by playing it." We find these same qualities exemplified where he explains why African nationalists are like they are and tells us that "we should treat them neither as saints nor as agitators," and "should not be disappointed when a nationalist turns out to be less than perfect."

His conception of the aims of British policy in Africa will come as a surprise to many who are not conversant with its history. Yet those who have watched the evolution of post-war British Colonial policy, so largely under Sir Andrew's influence, will not find his statement—"training the people to run their own countries has, I believe, been the main distinguishing characteristic of British administration in Africa"—out of line with what has been done. This has, of course, been easier in the West than in East and Central Africa; it is easier in Uganda than in Kenya and Southern Rhodesia, where there are large permanent European populations, which makes us realize that the steps between a declared policy and its realization may be many and difficult.

There are few questions asked about Africa today that Sir Andrew does not face up to. The oft-repeated query whether Africans are ready for independence has rarely been better put in perspective than in his assertion about newly independent peoples that "the social and economic problems that face them are not solved by independence, nor can the grant of independence be delayed until they have been solved." He stresses how important it is for the countries of the Western World to understand the extent of their stake in Africa, and what we must all do to help the newly independent countries that have come, and will shortly come, into being to achieve the position they must attain.

This book is thus significant not only for its exposition of past developments, and of the motivations and usages that underlay them, but also for its prediction of things to come and the ways they can be attained. In its pages, we come close to the African scene as it is, the problems it presents, the solutions it has achieved. Reading it will help us to better understand the new, dynamic Africa, and the questions its rapid pace of change pose for all who have sympathy with African aspirations and wish to know how best to be of aid to all concerned in making for their peaceful realization.

ADLAI E. STEVENSON

December, 1958

Preface

I greatly appreciated the invitation of the Harris Foundation Trustees to deliver the Harris Lectures at Northwestern University last April. Not only was it a very great honor to be asked; but this gave me the chance to look back on my experiences in African affairs during the last twenty-five years, and in doing so to analyze the causes underlying policies and events and to examine present needs and future opportunities.

We in Britain are proud of the transformation which we have helped the people of the African Territories to make during the last fifteen years; three of my talks deal with this period and with the future. But the rapid changes since the Second World War can be better understood against the background of what went before; in my first talk, therefore, I have touched briefly on the origins of our encounter with Africa and on the period of building in the fifty years before 1940.

Today the two main dynamic forces in the countries which we administer are African nationalist movements and British officials. Nationalism only started to make its weight felt in tropical Africa after the Second World War; we must recognize that it is the strongest human force of the twentieth century, and, if our policies are to succeed, we must work with the nationalists, as we have shown that we can do in many countries, both in Africa and elsewhere. British officials have been the spearheads of progress since British administration in Africa began. Too little is known in the United States, and even in Britain, about their work and their problems. I have dealt particularly with district

vii

staffs and Colonial Governors. District administration is the foundation of all government work in the African countries, and in this whole period Governors have largely held the keys to policy and progress.

I have ended these talks by discussing the gaps in the economy and social equipment of the African countries and the way in which the outside world can help to fill them. As political development goes forward and more and more countries achieve independence or approach it, I believe that our main task in dealing with these countries will be to settle with them the right way of giving this help. It will be a task in which the United States and Britain will have to work closely together with the African countries themselves and others concerned. To be successful in this common effort, we must understand each other, and I hope that this small book may achieve something in promoting this understanding in relation to African affairs.

These talks were delivered several months ago. I have not revised them to take account of political or other events which have occurred since. No mention, therefore, is made of the decisions taken at the Montreal Conference last September, when the Governments of the British Commonwealth expressed their determination to help the less developed parts of the Commonwealth maintain the progress of their development programs. Nor do I mention the agreement that Nigeria shall be independent in October, 1960, reached between the Nigerian leaders and the British Secretary of State for the Colonies at the London Conference in October.

The opinions I have expressed are not official pronouncements, but my own personal views. I should like to express my deep thanks to Professor Melville Herskovits of Northwestern University for his friendly stimulation. I am greatly indebted also to Dr. L. A. Fallers of the University of California and Mr. R. C. Pratt of McGill University; they are old friends from Uganda days, and their help was most fruitful when I was thinking out the material for these talks.

New York   ANDREW COHEN
December, 1958

Contents

III THE TASKS OF GOVERNMENT

IV AFRICA AND THE WEST: NEEDS OF THE FUTURE

British Policy in Changing Africa

ONE

Africa and the West: Encounter and Period of Building

I HAVE ATTENDED many ceremonies. None has moved me more that the Jubilee of Gayaza Girls' School which was held in 1955 in the heart of one of the richest parts of Buganda, some twelve miles north of Kampala. This is the leading girls' secondary school in Uganda, founded by the Church Missionary Society at the request of the Baganda Chiefs. The girls put on a pageant showing the first lady teachers walking eight hundred miles from the coast in the strange costumes devised to protect them from the sun and from insects. We saw the first girls brought by the Chiefs to the school, the loving care devoted by the teachers to the building up of Gayaza, and the deep affection which the Baganda girls gave them. And finally came the school tractor and cultivator driven on by the first Uganda woman graduate of a university in England, resplendent in her Oxford cap and gown. The tractor was for the school farm which is designed to help experiments in local diet. The woman was Miss Sarah Nyendwoha, a Munyoro, a history teacher and a young woman of character, public spirit, charm, wit, and sophistication—one of the friends in Uganda whom I most value. I relate the story first because it brings out one of the things which is most important in the history of African progress, the great missionary contribution, and secondly because it illustrates the most important need for Africa in the future, the emergence of leaders, both men and women—and above all women, because of the relative backwardness so far of girls' education and the small part played so far by women in public life.

More recently, in December, 1956, not long before I left Uganda, I took part in another ceremony of an entirely different kind. With the great backdrop of the Ruwenzori Mountains behind me I tightened the last fishplate of the western extension of the railroad and declared it open. I did so in front of a large and distinguished gathering of Rulers and Chiefs from Western Uganda and other parts of the country; ministers, politicians, and officials from Kampala and Entebbe; mining and businessmen from Britain and North America; and distinguished visitors of all races from neighboring countries, including the Vice Governor-General of the Belgian Congo. Afterwards the Omukama of Toro, the Ruler of that area, named the locomotive after his tribe.

We had come there in a ceremonial train from Kampala, speeded on our way by the Kabaka of Buganda, traveling first through the fertile, well-watered Buganda countryside, rich with cotton, coffee, and bananas, and peopled by prosperous Baganda yeomen farmers. Then through the night to the edge of the Toro escarpment, to see at dawn the whole range of the Ruwenzori with its snows shining in the morning sun. Stanley had been not far from where we were less than 70 years before and described the Mountains of the Moon in great detail. Many of the early travelers never saw them because, as often happens, they were shrouded in clouds. Herodotus talks of a snow mountain which travelers had seen somewhere near the sources of the Nile. We ran down the escarpment on a line looping over itself and then over the Lake George flats on a causeway built to carry the line; here I myself had the longed-for excitement of driving the train.

I mention the ceremony because of the connection of this whole area with the story of the early explorers, and because the railroad was vital to the establishment of the British connection with Uganda and also with Kenya and to the development, progress, and wealth of these two countries and their peoples. Uganda and Kenya, so different in their history in many respects, are both served by this lifeline to the coast. After monumental feats of construction under almost impossible conditions, the railroad reached Lake Victoria before the First World War and Kampala between the wars. Now it had been extended to Ruwenzori, a thousand miles from the coast, to serve the new copper mine at Kilembe in the folds of the mountains, to help enrich Western Buganda, Toro, and Ankole, and to provide a new line of communication with the Eastern Congo. The ceremony was not only a romantic occasion, but one which well illustrates the great building achievements of our early years in Africa. It illustrates also the need of these countries in the future for still more utilities and basic services, to help raise still further their wealth and the standards of their people.

I shall end up this series of talks by speaking of the help which the outside world can give the African countries in meeting needs such as this, of the challenge of Africa today to the world at large, and of the opportunity which this generation and the next have in relation to Africa. But before I come to that I want to say something about the political developments of recent years, the building up of new nations, and the interplay between nationalism and tribal loyalty; about African leaders and the problems which they face; about the contribution of British officers and their problems; and about our economic and educational policies in the last few years. I will deal with these things at a later stage. But I feel that first of all I must say something about the past. I am no historian, nor do I intend to turn these talks into a historical thesis. But I believe it will help to understand the mainsprings of British policy today if in this first talk I mention the most important influences which in the past have contributed to our present attitudes. So as not to have too wide a canvass I have decided to exclude the Central African Territories from my talks. I shall deal, therefore, with the West and East African territories which, with the Belgian Congo and the French territories of West and Equatorial Africa, may be said to form the middle tier of the continent.

THE ENCOUNTER

I will start my brief essay in history with a few things about what I will call the encounter of Africa with the Western world. What I say will perhaps be well known to many readers. I repeat these things only because they are necessary to the story.

The Abolition of Slavery

It was the discovery of America and the opening up by West European countries of colonies along the North, Central, and South American coasts and in the Caribbean which led directly, through the slave trade, to the association between the Western world and West Africa. America was developed with the help of West African slave labor; Europe was enriched by the trade. In the process the countries of Western Europe set up many trading centers on the West African coast. The Western world did not invent the slave trade; it had been practiced for many years before the wholesale transportation of slaves from West Africa across the Atlantic. But the Western world did turn the slave trade into big business.

After outstripping first the Dutch and then the French, Britain by the latter part of the eighteenth century had become the leading nation in the slave trade. It was in Britain also that the movement for abolition began in the late eighteenth century under the leadership of Wilberforce and other prominent men. And Britain through diplomatic action and naval force played the major part in the actual process of stamping out the slave trade. But it is important to bear in mind that Britain and the United States, along with other countries, worked in common over the long period which the process took. Sierra Leone was founded in 1787 by Britain through private initiative acting with the support of Government; Liberia was founded in 1816 by the United States through the American Colonization Society.

Later in the century the energy generated by the movement in the United States flowed into the domestic struggle for the abolition of slavery. In Britain the moral revulsion which prompted the anti-slavery campaign found expression later in movements to carry Western civilization into Africa, later still in movements to protect the people of Africa from undesirable exploitation in the very process of their growing contact with the Western world, and finally in the progressive policy developed during the present century—a policy which has had the support of the great majority of opinion in Britain in all political parties. The spirit of the anti-slavery movement is in fact enshrined in the evangelical tradition of Britain—a tradition which has found expression in a deep and practical concern for the welfare of have-nots overseas, a tradition kept alive by reformers, colonial administrators, and liberal societies. It is one which has increasingly colored the attitudes of public opinion in Britain.

Missions, Exploration, and Trade

The leaders of the anti-slavery movement saw that abolition was not enough; they looked to the spread of the Christian way of life and to the development of legitimate trade to repair the damage done by slavery. Hence came the founding of a series of missionary societies at the end of the eighteenth and the beginning of the nineteenth centuries. From this flowed the great and expanding missionary effort in West Africa, as well as in other parts of Africa, an effort which has not only gained many millions of converts to Christianity, but has also provided the main means of developing education in the African countries and an important agency for the extension of medical services. Education at the lower and middle levels is still to a very large extent conducted by or with the help of the missionary societies. Of course in all this the Catholic missions have played their full part as well as the Protestant societies. The contribution of missionaries to the progress of Africa cannot, I think, be fully grasped unless one has lived there, seen what they have built, and realized the leadership they have provided, the ideas and the moral values they have implanted and cultivated in these countries.

Trade with Africans was not felt by the humanitarians to be a form of exploitation, but just the reverse; they believed that it would help to liberate Africans. Here the Marxist and the liberal divide, for the liberal saw trade as benefiting both the trader and the people. The missionaries reinforced this Manchester School position with the belief that legitimate trade opportunities would help convert both slave traders and

African Chiefs from slave running and that the income from trade would be of great value as a lever to raise the people from a deep-rooted lethargy. It was the same motive which in a later period led administrators and agricultural officers to press cash crops on conservative peasants.

A knowledge of the interior of the West African countries was clearly indispensable for their development. The African Association was therefore founded in 1788 with the help of the abolitionists, and a series of expeditions into the interior followed, mainly in search of the Niger River and its course. There was a steadily increasing growth of genuine interest in West Africa and its people. Thus missionary activity, exploration of the interior, and trade went together. By the early 1860's the British Government had taken control of the trading establishments on the Gold Coast and in Nigeria. But this only happened after a long period of hesitation and controversy in Britain, with a series of commissions of inquiry and changes of policy by the Government. The whole period was in fact marked by a strong reluctance on the part of the British Parliament and Government to accept permanent responsibilities in West Africa. This was due partly to an intense dislike by Parliament of the financial responsibilities involved, partly to the theory, based on our experience in North America, that political control was not indispensable for the expansion of trade; and partly perhaps to the failure of the colony founded in Senegambia in the latter part of the eighteenth century, after the Senegal ports had been captured from the French. During this period abolitionists and missionaries as well as traders wanted a forward policy and pressed for increased British Government control so as to insure stability for their work.

The Partition of Africa

But generally speaking Britain did not assume political control in the interior until the French and Germans had started pursuing an active forward policy in West Africa—the French soon after 1870, the Germans by 1882. Britain assumed a protectorate over the Oil Rivers (the coast of Southern Nigeria) in 1885 and over Northern Nigeria through the Royal Niger Chartered Company from that year onwards. Control over the Gold Coast was completed by the end of the century.

The movement for the abolition of slavery did not lead immediately to the establishment of colonial rule; but once the movement was under way the process of stamping out the slave trade on the coast and in the interior, together with the expansion of trade and missionary activity which was itself a direct result of the anti-slavery campaign, led to a steadily increasing European involvement in West Africa. Other motives, both diplomatic and commercial, then entered the picture. Humanitarian aims, diplomatic rivalry, commercial interests—all three contributed to the partition of West Africa by Britain, France, and Germany. But, as far as Britain was concerned, it was the anti-slavery movement, the humanitarian factor, which led to the involvement from which all the rest followed.

East Africa

Similar developments took place in East Africa. Britain became closely involved in Zanzibar about the middle of the nineteenth century in the process of putting down the slave trade. This was followed by exploration of the interior, and the first European travelers, Speke and Grant, reached Buganda in 1862. In 1877 the first representatives of the British Church Missionary Society arrived, following Stanley's letter inviting missionaries to Buganda on behalf of Kabaka Mutesa. They were followed by French Catholic missionaries. At the same period there was an approach to the country from the north by Baker and later by Emin Pasha operating on behalf of the Khedive of Egypt; but this never effectively reached Buganda itself. I cannot deal here in detail with the complicated but stirring events which followed—the rivalries between the two groups of missionaries and between them jointly and the Arab traders, and the struggles between the rival factions among the Baganda of adherents of the two Christian Churches and of the Mohammedan religion which the Arabs had introduced.

The rivalries between the European powers culminated in 1890 in the appearance in Uganda of the German, Karl Peters. But in this year the British and German spheres of interest were agreed between the two Governments, leaving what are now Uganda and Kenya in the British sphere. Lugard was sent up to Buganda by the British East Africa Company; but in 1891 the Company decided that it could no longer afford the cost of maintaining itself there and the British Government at this time was most reluctant to assume protection. The strongest possible pressure was put on the Government by the missionary societies and by Lugard himself to reverse the decision to evacuate. There was a great campaign of meetings and resolutions throughout the United Kingdom. Eventually, after a report by a Special Commissioner sent to the country, Britain assumed protection in 1894. The protectorate over Uganda led automatically to a protectorate over what is now Kenya, since this was the only effective means of approach to Uganda.

The main element in the decision to stay in Uganda was the determination of the missionaries to be able to continue their work of spreading Christianity and civilization, and the support which they were able to secure in Britain from very large numbers of ordinary religious people. But the missionary effort might not have succeeded but for the rivalries between European nations over this African country which contained the source of the Nile. The interests of trade were a secondary motive only. Skepticism in Britain about the prospects of commercial expansion is illustrated by Labouchère's famous poem of 1896 about the Uganda Railway:

> *What it will cost no words can express;*
>   *What is its object no brain can suppose;*
> *Where it will start from no one can guess;*
>   *Where it is going to nobody knows.*
>
> *What is the use of it none can conjecture;*
>   *What it will carry there's none can define;*
> *And in spite of George Curzon's superior lecture,*
>   *It clearly is naught but a lunatic line.*

Reflections on the Encounter

Before I leave this period I would like to make some general comments about it. Modern opinion usually regards the partition of Africa as a discreditable episode in world history. It is true that rivalry between the European powers played a large part in the process. It is true that the methods used in securing the agreement of African Chiefs to the assumption of protection were often questionable. It is true that the economic interests of the metropolitan countries were a factor in promoting this policy, although less so in West and East Africa than in the Congo and the Rhodesias. It is easy to see why modern opinion should take an adverse view of these operations.

But we need, I believe, to be more cautious in forming a final judgment. There is another side to the picture and an important one. In West and East Africa the economic interests of European companies and countries, although they entered into the picture, were not the major motive or even the first in the field; not all the arguments of Marxist historians can make me believe that they were. The abolition of slavery and, in revulsion from the slave trade, the sense of mission toward the people of Africa were the first motives in time in the British penetration of both West and East Africa. The promotion of trade was part of the program of the abolitionists, and the strength of the economic incentive steadily grew as time went on. It may well be that neither of these motives would have prevailed against the caution, parsimony, and reluctance to be involved of a large section of public and parliamentary opinion in Britain had it not been for the rivalry with other European nations—itself of course partly commercial. It may well be that without this we should not have established colonial rule in these areas. But, given that we did, the humanitarian origins of our entry into Africa have left their mark on all that has happened since.

The assumption and consolidation of European control over tropical Africa involved some violence; it also involved some incidents and policies which are discreditable by any standards, particularly in relation to modern values. But compared with similar processes at other periods of history and in other parts of the world it was, with some glaring exceptions, peaceable, orderly, and humanitarian. Certainly it involved less violence than the corresponding process in America. European penetration and control of tropical Africa was in general followed by a long period of peaceful and constructive progress for the people of these countries. During the period many trading concerns from overseas made money—a fact which seems to some people shocking in a colonial setting, though self-evident and desirable in the opening up of a new country like the United

States. But remember that this money was not made by governments, as the old-fashioned anti-colonialist tends to believe, but by traders of enterprise and determination, operating with very little state assistance and bringing in the wake of their activity great advances in the standard of living of the African people. Who is to say that these people were "exploiters" and not "pioneers"? In less than three generations regions which were very backward, particularly in their material development, have been transformed. Less than a hundred years after the southern part of the Gold Coast came under British control, that country has been brought to nationhood. Could these things have been done except through a colonial regime? I know of no serious critic who has established that the same results could have been achieved without the assumption of outside control.

THE PERIOD OF BUILDING

I now turn to the period from the 1890's to the beginning of the Second World War. This is the period of building—fifty years of steady and unspectacular development interrupted only by the First World War and the slump of the 1930's. Administrative control was extended over the whole of the Territories; law, order, and justice were firmly established; government services and institutions were built up and brought into full operation; local government was developed mainly through the system of indirect rule; and the foundations were laid for the growth of central political institutions.

Schools and medical services were developed to the extent that the resources of the Territories allowed. The period included great achievements such as the virtual eradication of human sleeping sickness in Uganda. Towns were built up and, by malaria control, made healthy places to live in. But over most of the period conditions were in many places unhealthy. Blackwater, yellow fever and other diseases took their heavy toll. The graveyard outside Namirembe Cathedral in Kampala contains the simple graves of many pioneers in missionary and government work, and of others who were stricken down as young men when they were just starting to serve these countries. This period was indeed a time of pioneers, of great individualists who have left a lasting mark on these countries and who will not be forgotten by the African people: men like Ainsworth, Chief Native Commissioner in Kenya; Simpson, Director of Agriculture in Uganda; later, Dundas, Provincial Commissioner in Northern Tanganyika.

Roads, railroads, and ports were built to give access to the interior of the Territories. Economic crops were introduced or developed: groundnuts, palm oil, and cocoa in West Africa; cotton, coffee, tea, and sisal in East Africa. In West Africa and mainly in Uganda these were African peasant crops; in Kenya they were mostly produced by European farmers or plantations; in Tanganyika by a mixture of the two. Tin mines were started in Nigeria and gold, bauxite, and manganese mines in the Gold Coast. Trade and commerce developed steadily, and the pioneering efforts of Europeans in private business enterprise are one of the most important achievements of this period. In East Africa also Indian traders played a valuable part in economic development by carrying trade, and cotton ginning in Uganda, to the remoter parts of these countries.

The most striking years for development were those from 1895 onwards, when Mr. Joseph Chamberlain was Secretary of State for the Colonies. Railroads were built from the coast in Sierra Leone, the Gold Coast, and Nigeria as well as from Mombasa in Kenya. A very important measure by Mr. Chamberlain was the giving of trustee status to loans raised by colonial governments on the London market under the Colonial Stock

Act of 1900; this made possible large expenditure of loan funds for economic development in Africa and elsewhere. The administration of Mr. Amery after the First World War is notable for its encouragement both of scientific research and of economic development generally. These two men, usually regarded as imperialists, made a very special contribution to this period of building.

Financial Self-Sufficiency

It must be admitted that the process of rapid economic advance during the whole period was impeded by shortage of finance; that is not to say that substantial assistance was not given by the British Government both in loans and grants. But as a general principle the African Territories, like other Colonial Territories, were expected to be self-supporting financially. Grants-in-aid from the British Treasury were given if local revenue could not meet the necessary local expenditure; but deliberate budgeting for a deficit was not allowed.

It goes without saying of course that no revenue from the Territories was paid into the British Exchequer. Some Territories were able to meet considerable development expenditure from their own resources during the period. The Gold Coast under Guggisberg's Government in the 1920's was one of these; the port of Takoradi was opened and Achimota College established. Some Territories on the other hand were perennially short of money for development; all, but particularly the poorer ones, were gravely embarrassed during the slump of 1930. Tanganyika is perhaps the most striking example; it was only after the Second World War that the damage done by the 1930 slump began to be repaired. The shortage of Government money made all the more important the part which, as I have explained, private enterprise played in development throughout the period.

Critics of the system of financial self-sufficiency would say that without a sufficient capital investment in basic utilities, which in colonial conditions are unlikely to attract private enterprise, it is not possible to put a new country firmly on the path of economic advance. And equally that without assistance in the early stages for expanding government services, including education and medical services, it is not possible to bring the indigenous people into development and public life at an early enough stage. Supporters of the system claim that expanding services must be firmly based on growing local revenues, and that part of the process of growing toward political independence is to acquire the habit of financial self-sufficiency. No one would dispute this last point. But more recent experience throughout the world has shown the need for outside economic help even to more advanced countries; and also that this can be granted without detracting from the local sense of responsibility. There are few who would now deny that it would have made a great difference to the progress of the African Territories if financial assistance from Britain for economic and social development had been available at a much earlier stage on the scale provided since the beginning of the Second World War. As it is, limited assistance was provided for economic projects in 1929, when the British Parliament set aside a total of £1 million a year under the Colonial Development Act for all Colonial Territories together.

International and British Public Opinion

The somewhat negative approach toward the financing of colonial development was matched to a large extent by international opinion in the whole of this period and by public opinion generally in Britain. The Berlin Act of 1885 had laid down that traders, missionaries, and other agents of all countries should have free access to the interior of Africa, and in particular that navigation on the Congo and Niger rivers should be free to people of all nations. This arrangement sprang primarily from the belief that no nation should obtain an unfair advantage over others through control over colonies or protectorates. No doubt also the framers of the Berlin Act, brought up in the doctrine of laissez faire, genuinely believed that complete free trade, rather than deliberate and constructive measures for development, was the best way of promoting the economic advancement of the whole region. Whether this has in fact proved to be the case, and whether in actual practice complete equality has been preserved, is a matter for argument. Apart from this the Berlin and Brussels Acts prohibited the trade in arms to Africans to keep the peace and help stamp out the slave trade and intertribal fighting, and the trade in spiritous liquor whether by importation or local distillation. This latter provision was of course introduced with the highest motives, but the ban on importation has encouraged the production of far more noxious local products which it has been impossible effectively to control.

I mention this only to illustrate the tendency during this whole period on the part of progressive opinion to concentrate on the prohibition of abuses rather than on positive and constructive action for development. Progressive societies in Britain tended to take the same line. Of course they did valuable and indeed indispensable work in campaigning for such important matters as the protection of African land rights and the prevention of bad labor conditions. But there was more insistence by progressive opinion, both British and international, on safeguarding African society than on helping Africans to develop and stimulating the inertia which tended to prevail among the people of many parts of Africa. As one who knew the British Colonial Office toward the end of this period only, I would say that in some parts of that institution the same attitude was to be found even in the early 1930's. I have heard it described by an aggressive critic as the woad policy; no doubt unjustified, but with a grain of truth in it. It began to change during the 1930's both inside and outside the official world. Going back to the early 1920's it is noteworthy that the League of Nations mandates contained far more provisions against abuse than in favor of positive action. The United Nations Trusteeship Agreements, negotiated in a most constructive period after the Second World War, contain firm obligations on administering powers to promote the political, economic, social, and educational advance of the Territories and their people.

Constitutional Growth in West Africa

I have suggested earlier that financial self-sufficiency and outside assistance are not incompatible. Financial self-sufficiency as such is inherent in the whole British approach to overseas Territories, that of building them up as units separate from Britain and with their own budgets and legislative and administrative institutions. This was the practice followed in the American colonies, and indeed the American colonists would have tolerated nothing less. The British experience in America before independence no doubt taught those in authority in Britain to respect colonial opinion. The same practice was followed in other parts of the world, including Africa. In West Africa the inhabitants had no experience of democratic institutions on Western lines. But Legislative Councils had been set up in all these countries by the early part of the second half of the nineteenth century. At first they consisted only of British officials. Soon afterwards people from outside Government were included; at first these were British traders and missionaries, but by the end of the century some educated Africans had been added.

After the First World War Nigeria, Sierra Leone, and the Gold Coast were all granted a substantial constitutional advance. The legislatures still had official majorities, but with a majority of Africans on the unofficial side and with some of these elected, mostly by the towns on a limited franchise, in the Gold Coast also by the Joint Provincial Council of Chiefs established in the Colony. In Nigeria the scope of the Legislature did not cover the Northern Provinces; in the Gold Coast it covered neither Ashanti nor the Northern Territories. Until the war there were no Africans on the Governors' Executive Councils. The advance, though substantial, was a cautious one, more important for the future than for what it was at that time, important in fact for the form and pattern which it created.

East African Constitutions

In East Africa the course of constitutional advance was different, although parallel. In Kenya European settlement had been officially encouraged since 1900 so as to produce economic development along the railroad from Mombasa in country which was largely uninhabited except for the nomadic Masai. Europeans were to make a decisive contribution to the development of the country. In 1906 a Legislative Council was set up with a small number of non-government Europeans on it. During the First World War election for Europeans was introduced, with the official majority still retained; and, after a long controversy as to numbers, some Asians were added in 1927 and one nominated European member to represent African interests—a second was added some ten years later. After the First World War non-

government members were added to the Governor's Executive
Council: two Europeans, one Asian, and one European to represent African interests. No African was included in the Legislative
Council until the Second World War. Small Legislative Councils with a minority of unofficial Europeans and Asians were
established during the 1920's in Uganda and Tanganyika; there
were no Africans on these bodies during this period.

In Kenya we see the meeting of two principles of British
policy: the first was the development of parliamentary government by the local immigrant communities, the only people who
at that stage could have exercised it in that area; the second was
the principle of trusteeship on behalf of the African inhabitants.
The first principle had operated in the southern part of Africa
and was continued in 1923 in Southern Rhodesia after the end
of the Chartered Company's administration there. Southern
Rhodesia—that is, the European inhabitants of Southern Rhodesia—were given at that time responsible government in internal
affairs, with a veto reserved to the United Kingdom Government on legislation differentiating between Europeans and
Africans. In Kenya, as later in Northern Rhodesia, the Europeans
were given and have since retained a very influential position.
The political philosophy of most Europeans in Kenya at that
time was based on the maintenance of control by the white
community. But there were comparatively few of them, I believe, who would actually have welcomed being entrusted with
the government of the country. The British Government in any
case did not hand over the government to them. Indeed much
energy was devoted during the 1920's to working out the guiding principle on which Kenya should be governed and developed, and much irritation and misunderstanding was generated
on this subject.

A Conservative Secretary of State for the Colonies in 1923
and later a Labour Secretary of State in 1930 enunciated the
principle of paramountcy of African interests. This aroused

much controversy until eventually a Joint Select Committee of both Houses of the British Parliament laid down in 1931 that the term meant that the interests of the African majority should not be subordinated to those of any minority, however important. This pronouncement clearly settled nothing; and the measure of inconsistency between the dominion and the trusteeship policies remained unresolved. Meanwhile, however, the advancement of Africans was going forward steadily in all fields and, with the emergence of considerable numbers of educated and politically minded Africans in Kenya, it is now possible for the future relationship between the different races there to be worked out largely by them on the spot, with the British Government as the arbiter with ultimate authority—a process which I venture to think is a healthier one and, in spite of its difficulty, a more hopeful one for the future.

Indirect Rule

Finally I must say something about the policy of indirect rule, which figured so large in this whole period. Indirect rule, governing in local affairs through the customary institutions of the people of the area, fits into the general British conception of relying on local institutions rather than a centralized bureaucracy. But it was not a policy laid down from London; it was introduced and has since been developed largely as a result of local initiative. Lugard introduced it in Northern Nigeria in the first years of the century, going there with too few administrators for a system of direct rule and finding well organized and in some cases large and powerful Emirates through which he could work. In some respects the structure of these Emirates was similar to what he had already seen in Buganda. Both depended on a local bureaucracy deriving authority from the Ruler, the Emir in Northern Nigeria and the Kabaka in Buganda. The Ruler in fact exercised direct rule over his subjects and it was only in the relationship between the Ruler and the British Governor and his Administration that indirect rule was involved.

The system of indirect rule was applied in Western Nigeria in 1916 and in Tanganyika when Britain took over the administration, in substitution of the direct rule operated by the Germans. Later it was applied to Eastern Nigeria, Sierra Leone, Northern Rhodesia, Nyasaland, and Ashanti and the Northern Territories of the Gold Coast. During the 1920's Sir Donald Cameron set out in a series of classical memoranda the principles of indirect rule as he applied them in Tanganyika to the political side of native administration, to court work, and to the setting up of native administration treasuries.

To ascertain the customary tribal authorities in areas where no clearly recognizable traditional authority was already established it was often necessary to carry out elaborate inquiries, sometimes with the assistance of anthropologists. The Native Authority recognized by Government was normally the Chief, but sometimes it was the Chief in Council, the Chief and Council, or simply a Council; where the Chief alone was recognized a system of advisers to the Chief was usually part of the system, but these advisers were normally not constituted as part of the Native Authority. In many areas, in order to follow tradition, large numbers of Native Authorities had to be recognized. There were about 400 in Tanganyika, but it was found possible later to federate many of these, so that the number of Native Treasuries is only about 50. In large areas, notably parts of Tanganyika, Eastern Nigeria, and even the pagan parts of Northern Nigeria itself, the Native Authorities were so small and so backward as to be able to do little as units of local administration. With such Authorities we were a long way from the Emirates or the Buganda Kingdom.

In areas where there was a firm traditional foundation to

build on, indirect rule served the Territories well. Because it functioned through machinery broadly familiar to them it was a good means of contact between the people and the Government. It carried the people with reasonable smoothness through a period of substantial if slow and sometimes almost imperceptible change and adjustment. It was the medium through which many individual British officers, often men of remarkable character and great devotion to the people they worked with, were able to exercise their qualities of leadership in guiding the people forward. Indeed it provided just the kind of local flexibility which gave men of this type good scope. Indirect rule, moreover, laid the foundations of local government and sometimes more than the foundations. Generally speaking, except in Northern Nigeria, the Native Authorities did not themselves undertake the responsibility for operating local services, such as hygiene or soil conservation services. But they did act as a channel through which the officers of the Central Government both administrative and technical, could explain and put across new policies and plans for the welfare and progress of the people.

To a very large extent, except in the fairly limited areas where Chiefs were educated and progressive, the Government officers had to take the initiative themselves, just as in Native Authority finance the administrative officers had in most cases to do most of the work over the local estimates, particularly in the early stages. But in most cases the process was educative and produced practical results, if very often gradually. It operated through the Chiefs, but as under native custom the Chiefs normally did not express views or take action without consultation with traditional elders or advisers, the effect in areas where indirect rule was operating in a classical manner was to give reasonable assurance that consultation and cooperation with the people was genuine. At the same time, where there was opposition to government measures and plans, the system provided a smooth and reasonably effective method of bringing this to the notice of the government officers concerned. Sometimes of course this process of consultation did not work as it was intended to do, particularly where, as happened in some cases, the influence of elders and counselors had atrophied following the Government's recognition of the Chief as the sole Native Authority.

Unfortunately there were large areas where the foundations of indirect rule in the classical pattern were not firm, where, as I have said, the units were too small or the traditional leadership too weak, even if it existed at all, to provide an effective foundation for local administration or, at a later stage, local government. In so far as indirect rule did not succeed in many areas, this was to a large extent the cause. Why was the system applied in these areas with too meticulous an insistence on the discovery and recognition of the traditional Chiefs or other authorities? Why was it not suitably adapted to the circumstances of these areas? Was this due to too rigid an approach by governments? Partly, perhaps: all bureaucratic systems are rigid and, having accepted and absorbed an idea, tend to stick to it too tenaciously. The *mystique* of indirect rule *pur sang* was pretty strong. Was it because of any centralized laying down of policy from Whitehall? An element of this probably entered into the picture; particularly during the 1930's the Colonial Office was generally encouraging governments in Africa which had not done so to introduce the system. But I do not think that centralized direction was the cause to any large extent. The Colonial Office always to a large degree left things to the government concerned in matters of native administration.

The real answer is, I believe, largely this: the method of applying indirect rule was based on the assumption that we had indefinite time ahead during which the system could grow and develop under our guidance—an assumption accepted without question at the time by almost everybody. We were in fact building on what was found to exist in each area, adapting this gradually to the needs of administration and progress and purging it of its undesirable or repugnant features, but essentially adapting it rather than imposing something totally new and unfamiliar from outside. The belief was that by amalgamations, federations, and the building up of larger units, and by the emergence in greater numbers of educated and competent Chiefs and native administration officials, the system would gradually become more effective and more suited to modern needs.

The Belief in Indefinite Time Ahead

The belief that we had indefinite time perhaps partly explains another point: why the system of indirect rule was not adapted more quickly and effectively to the needs of the growing towns. The criticism has commonly been made by politically minded Africans and others that indirect rule as it was usually applied was unsuited to the towns and did not provide satisfactorily for the growing numbers of people who congregated there, and that in particular it did not give a proper outlet to the growing numbers of educated people, to the professional men when they appeared and to the African middle class. There was, I am sure, also another reason for these things; indirect rule was essentially an administrative system, designed by administrators to deal with people living under tribal conditions, their problems, their relations with the central government, their well-being, and their advancement. Since the vast majority of the people were living under rural conditions, it is not entirely surprising that the system took the form suited to these conditions. It was, moreover, a system which looked at the prob-

lems and interests of each given area or tribe. It was not con-
ceived in the framework of building up a state or a nation; still
less—and this is very natural—did it take into account the
tendencies and pressures appearing in the world at large, which
at a later stage were to affect tropical Africa.

The objective of self-government was, of course, generally
accepted during this period by those concerned with the African
territories; but by most individuals it was regarded as something for the pretty remote future which did not affect im-
mediate policies and plans. This may be the reason why no
attempt was made in the period before the Second War to use
the central political institutions to knit Nigeria or the Gold Coast
together as a country, by giving each of them a Legislature
covering the whole country and by bringing Africans onto
the Governor's Executive Council: and why in East Africa
attempts were not made to devise—or at any rate to prepare
for—some kind of central political machinery which would
represent the Africans as well as the immigrant communities. These things would have been difficult to do at the
time and there was no strong demand for them among the
people of the countries concerned. That they were not done is
certainly not to be taken as a sign that there was not enough
concern in the Governments or the Colonial Office for African
advancement. On the contrary, this was the main concern both
of the Colonial Office and the local administrations. It was not
that; rather it was the assumption that we had indefinite time
that led to these things being left until a later period.

The same is to a large extent true of the principle of financial self-sufficiency. Of course, as I have explained, this
was inherent in the whole British policy towards overseas territories in Africa and elsewhere. But its application to these
poor and undeveloped areas in Africa, and the fact that it
was not modified to any substantial extent for Africa at an
earlier stage than the Second World War, was again, I be-

lieve, due to the assumption that there was indefinite time ahead. Given time, the export crops which had been developed, the mines which had been opened, the communications which had been built, the education and health services which were being extended could be allowed gradually to increase the national wealth and government revenue of these countries. Had it been possible to foresee in the period between the wars how soon political development at the center of these countries would go rapidly forward, it seems more than possible at any rate that steps might have been taken at an earlier stage than they were to make special financial assistance available on a large scale to the Territories for economic and social development.

IN SUMMARY

There is a great deal of hindsight in all that I have been saying, and I do not want to be thought to be undervaluing in any sense the achievement of this whole period from the end of the nineteenth century up to 1940. To do so would be as impertinent as it would be unjustified. The transformation which was achieved in these fifty years was remarkable. The numbers of British officers and other British people living and working in the African Territories was relatively small. They were working under great physical limitations and in a world of laissez-faire. To them must go the major credit for the great achievements of this period. Hindsight about the policies of the period is justified only in analyzing the reasons for them. There is a tendency in some quarters to look upon this whole period as if it were almost in the Dark Ages. This is utterly wrong; it was a period of steady enlightenment and progress. In talking about it we must remember that it was not only those in government, whether in Africa or Britain, who based their attitudes and actions on the assumption that there was indefinite time ahead. Until the War there would have been very few people anywhere who would have questioned this, even, I believe, in the United States. And, as I have already said, international opinion during this period tended to be more concerned with the protection of the people of the African Territories from abuses or wrong exploitation than with the problems of building up African nations.

My next talk will be concerned with the new policy in Britain towards African development, both economic and educational; the attempts to modernize native administration; the rapid constitutional advance of the Territories; the emergence of nationalism as an active force; and the building up of nations in Africa. But I have one final point which leads up to these later events. In the field of administration and politics indirect rule held the main part of the stage before 1940. The energy of the administrative service in the Territories went largely into this. It was something quite new in British action overseas. It had not been practiced in India; the Indian Princely States were largely left to govern themselves in internal affairs. But at the same time as indirect rule, and indeed even before it, the classic British principle of building up overseas territories as separate units with their own finances and their own Legislatures had been applied both in West and East Africa. During the period before 1940 the central political institutions of the Territories were not given anything like a fully representative character. Yet the fact that they were set up was of supreme importance for the future. Once Legislative Councils were making the laws and controlling the finances of these Territories, even though the elected element in them was small or did not exist at all, it was inevitable that, as education and economic development bore their fruit in the growing awareness of the people, there would be demands for more representation, more widespread systems of election—ultimately for an effective part in the Central Government itself.

The pattern of the old Dominions was there for all who had any considerable degree of education to see, and as communications with the outside world became easier it was inevitable that the idea of self-government on Western lines should gain currency in Africa, just as many other Western ideas had. It was after all the proclaimed ideal for Africa of British statesmen. Thus, while much less attention was given to the growth of central institutions than to local administration during the period, the adoption of central institutions on the pattern of the rest of the British world, with all that this implied, was surely, and I believe inevitably, destined to play the major part in the end in shaping the future of these countries as it has of countries in other parts of the world.

TWO

The Nation and the Tribe

THE NEW POLICY AND ITS CAUSES

DURING THE Second World War British colonial policy acquired a completely new look. What did this consist of?

Colonial Development and Welfare

First, there was the new positive and constructive policy of economic and social development. Under the Colonial Development and Welfare Acts a total sum of $600 million has been made available by the British Government over the fifteen years up to 1960 for economic and social projects in all British dependent Territories, not only those in Africa. This is a very large sum of money in terms of colonial finance. It may seem small by the standards of this country; but remember that is was designed to prime the pump. It was greatly supplemented by loans raised by the Governments of the Territories on the London market, in effect with the guarantee of the British Government; by local surplus funds and revenue of the Territories; by private investment; and by the large investments of the Colonial Development Corporation financed by the British Government. Since the war about $3 billion has gone from Britain to the dependent Territories.

After the war every African Government drew up a comprehensive development program. There was in fact a great forward drive in education (including higher education), health programs, research, road building, the provision of water supplies, the cooperative movement, and in agricultural, mining, and industrial development. I shall have something to say about these things in a later talk.

New Local Government Policy

Secondly, there was the new local government policy enunciated by the Secretary of State in 1947. This was aimed at converting the system of indirect rule into an efficient, representative, and modern system of local government. The general object was to remedy some of the weaknesses which had shown themselves in the old system. Small and inefficient units were to be combined and merged into new bodies of a reasonable size, often on a district basis, and new local government bodies set up in the towns adapted to town conditions and representation. The educated people and the rising middle class, as well as the peasants, were to be given a more effective say in local government by the use of elections. The procedure of local government was to be adapted to modern needs. Local government bodies were to be given the chance to play a part in social and economic progress by gradually transferring to them control of local services such as primary education and rural health services. At the same time they were to be given access to more finance by a regular system of grants from the Central Government, by loans raised from or through the Central Government, and by encouraging them to make local taxation a progressive instrument by means of graduated poll taxes.

Generally speaking it was easier to introduce the new system in areas such as Kenya and parts of Uganda where indirect rule had not been applied on the Northern Nigeria-Tanganyika model. District Councils often already existed in these areas; these proved capable in a number of cases of taking over some local services, and they were relatively easy to make more representative by the introduction of elections. On the other hand where the units of native administration were very large, as in the Buganda Kingdom and the large Emirates of Northern Nigeria, the objective of introducing local government at levels below these bodies was much more difficult. In fact not much progress has been made, since both the Buganda Government and the Emirates have so far proved too centralized to allow of any effective devolution of local government powers.

Constitutional Advance

The third feature of the new look—and the most spectacular and most important—was the policy of constitutional advance. First, over-all legislatures were established, in West Africa covering the whole of each country, and in East Africa by bringing Africans onto the Legislative Councils. Secondly, the popular element on the Councils became steadily larger, and elections were introduced or extended and made direct. Thirdly, the popular element in the Governors' Executive Councils was steadily increased and, later, ministerial systems were established. In West Africa this has already carried Ghana to independence and the different regions of Nigeria and also Sierra

Leone to internal self-government in some cases or in others to something very like it. In East Africa what previously were purely official administrations, with Europeans and Asians drawn from the public playing only an advisory or critical role, have been turned into something quite different—ministries with men drawn from the public in them, including or shortly to include Africans, and much more representative Legislatures in which Africans are playing a substantial and growing part. The essential purpose of this policy, as of the new local government policy, was to train the people in responsibility by progressively giving them more powers.

Much in fact has happened during the last fifteen years. In West Africa the period of colonial rule has virtually ended. East Africa is still at a substantially earlier stage; but the political scene there has radically altered. What were the reasons for these great changes? What produced this new policy—new, that is, not in content but in emphasis and speed of application?

Reasons for the New Policy

First of all, before the war there were clear signs of change from the old laissez-faire attitude. Lord Hailey's *African Survey* had shown the need for a more positive approach to many problems. The West India Royal Commission of 1938, by setting out in clear form the facts of poverty and the backwardness of social services in the Caribbean, had aroused Parliament—and not only in relation to the West Indies. Progressive societies in Britain had been addressing themselves to the more positive needs. All this bore fruit in the Colonial Development and Welfare Act of 1940, passed during the Battle of Britain—a great act of faith.

Secondly, the war had brought new ideas. It was not only

the great contribution in manpower and resources made by the dependent Territories to the war effort which carried weight. It was something even bigger than that. There was the general feeling that the world should be put to rights, that richer and older nations should help people who were poor and under-developed to build themselves into new nations. It was, in fact, the policy of the Atlantic Charter.

Thirdly, there was the growth of nationalism. In West Africa nationalism was of course a factor in the political scene well before the war; but it grew very greatly and rapidly during and after the war. In East Africa nationalism did not appear in an organized form until the 1950's. But the 1945 and 1949 disturbances in Buganda were caused by frustrated and discontented elements operating in an atmosphere of economic grievance—a typical cause of nationalism. In Kenya also there were nationalist groups operating in the 1940's.

Nationalism

American observers more versed in political science than I have written with great insight about the growth of nationalist movements in Africa. I shall have a little to say about nationalists later; here I will give only a few blinding glimpses of the obvious. Nationalism in West Africa owes its origins, as do many other new things, to the impact of the West. This has brought Western ideas, above all the idea of progress; education, which supplied knowledge of the outside world and the desire for those political systems which the Western world so highly values; and economic development, which on the one hand through the introduction of commerce and industry helped to break down the old African societies and on the other raised large sections of the people above the subsistence level and helped to create a middle class, the traditional source of nationalist activity. All these things formed one of the elements in the birth of nationalism. The other was the intense and burning desire to be equal—not only as individuals, but as nations—bred of the history of Africa, but still more of grievances or imagined grievances against the colonial system. All these factors were intensified by closer contacts with the outside world—the experience of soldiers who went to fight abroad; the increasing numbers of students who after the War went to Europe and North America; the greatly increased flow of books and publications of all sorts bringing new political ideas into Africa; the success of nationalist movements in other parts of the world; the increasing strength of progressive opinion in Britain with its questioning of the existing state of affairs.

Those of us who speak of British policy sometimes attribute the great advances Britain has been making in Africa and elsewhere solely to our own wisdom, and I must plead guilty to having done this on occasion. We sometimes talk as if what governments do is solely due to a process of sitting down in an office or council chamber in London or abroad, thinking out what is right, and then doing it.

On the other hand, nationalists tend to attribute all reforms and progress to their own successful struggle for freedom. I have even seen this tendency in some learned articles by American scholars; no doubt it was their natural sympathy for nationalists which led them to overlook the other side of the picture.

Interrelated Pressures

The truth is that constitutional progress has depended on neither the action of governments nor on the pressure of local opinion, but on both. It has taken place as a result of what I propose to call interrelated pressures—on the one hand the pressure exerted through the actions and policies of the British Government, the Governments in the Territories, and public and parliamentary opinion in Britain, and on the other the pressure of nationalist and other opinions and attitudes in the Territories themselves. These pressures are of course not necessarily always exerted against each other; often they are complementary. Sometimes one or the other is, so to speak, in the ascendant, and it then supplies the motive force. Things work best when they are both operating effectively.

In the early stages the pressure of local opinion tends to be weak and unorganized and, if the official attitude is rigid or negative, progress may be slow or nonexistent. In such cases action by Government is often needed to induce movement forward by doing something which primes the political pump. Governors call this "keeping one step in front of public opinion." In the later stages of political advance pressure by nationalist forces tends to be strong and here, if Government is rigid, there may be an explosion, or, if Government is weak, progress may be too rapid or in the wrong direction. In fact, where local political forces or movements are powerful, smooth political progress depends on imagination as well as firmness on the part of governments, not only on strength but on flexibility.

From all this I would draw three conclusions. First, to respond to local political pressures is not a sign of weakness on the part of governments, as some critics sometimes suggest—they call it giving way to local agitation—but an ordinary process in political advance. Secondly, timetables for political advance, so popular with some members of the United Nations, who call them "target dates," do not fit in well with this theory of interrelated pressures. The working out of these pressures is an infinitely complicated process of relations between groups of human beings. The interaction of pressures may appear on

paper to be a less sure method than timetables; it may sometimes produce results which were unexpected and rates of progress which were not anticipated. But at least it has the advantage of moving step by step in consultation with local public
opinion and basing each step on the foundation of the one which
went before. Single short-term targets for a stage of advance in
a particular field may be a useful form of pressure by Governments to stimulate advance. But a series of successive targets
is hardly compatible with the theory of pressures, on which I
believe British practice to be based.

Thirdly, it is the late stages of political advance which are
the most delicate and difficult both for Governments and
nationalist leaders. During these stages particularly great caution
ought, I believe, to be shown by outside people or groups about
intervening between Governments and local public opinion.
Where local political forces are already strong, the balance
may be upset if outside opinion throws its weight purely on
their side—a danger which should be apparent to anybody ob-
serving the operations of some members of the Fourth Committee of the United Nations General Assembly in relation to
the French and British Cameroons. I refer to those who always
agree with petitioners before the United Nations because they
are petitioners and always disagree with Administering Authorities because they are Administering Authorities. A West
African once said: "The worst insult you in Britain give us
Africans is always to agree with us." I wish he had said it at
the United Nations.

Pressures within Britain and within the Territories

There is one final point regarding this theory. The pressures
on each side are not of course simple; they are very complex. On

one side there is opinion inside the Territorial Government, opinion which is by no means monolithic, and the Colonial Office, removed from local pressures and tending to take a longer view. In Britain there is progressive opinion, which covers nowadays a large segment of the political spectrum; there are those who are in general opposed to change, or at any rate to rapid change; and there are extremists on both sides of political opinion. There are commercial, industrial, and mining interests; the press in all its variety; those who follow African affairs in the universities; people having close links with European settlers; the missionary societies; and those with experience of colonial government.

Public opinion in the Territories is at least as complex because it covers everybody, not only, as in Britain, people interested in Africa. There are the nationalist politicians, both extreme and moderate; and the vernacular press, mostly linked with political groups. There may be political groups which are purely tribal; there are the traditionalists, the Chiefs, counselors, elders, and all who depend on the maintenance of the power of the Chiefs. There are the educated and professional men; the propertied middle class; the cooperative movement; the small traders; the trade unionists; the relatively well-to-do peasant farmers; the subsistence peasants—many of them uneducated. There are the different church groups—Protestants, Catholics and Muslims. Finally, there are the members of other races: white missionaries; commercial, industrial, mining, and professional men; and, in East Africa, farming settlers; also in East Africa, Asian businessmen and industrialists.

One thing is clear: the different groups on each side do not all exert pressure together. Some elements of local opinion may be ranged with the Government on some issues, whether they are African or not. It should not be assumed that, because the upper levels of Government have been largely manned by Europeans, therefore Europeans outside the Government would normally side with it. The experience of East Africa shows that this is not so. Among the African groups the nationalist, the traditional, and the modern professional and middle-class elements do not always exert pressure together. On the contrary, any one or more of these groups may be ranged with or against the Government on any issue or group of issues.

The interaction of pressures between the different groups in a Territory is in fact a major factor in local politics. It is important, therefore, that, to enable the different sections of public opinion to make their weight felt, all should be effectively represented politically. If any group is not so represented, Government has to take upon itself the responsibility of trying to safeguard its interests, and this is often an unsatisfactory method of operation. Both the lack of adequate representation in Legislative Councils of educated and politically minded elements in West Africa in the past and the limited effective representation of the traditional elements prior to independence in the Gold Coast led to trouble. In East Africa there were no African members of Legislative Councils until after the war, and it was only fairly recently that African representation was increased to a size where the members could be effectively in touch with their constituents. Before that African pressures had to be exerted in other ways, mostly through the contacts between Native Authorities or African Local Authorities and the Administration.

I do not say that this method was not effective, but its operation in central politics was inevitably filtered, usually through a series of filters. There could be no interpressure at the center between Africans and other races. Government, which was subject to pressure by other races in the Legislature, had to take responsibility for African pressure, and in effect to bring pressure on itself through the interchange between the African Affairs Branch and other sections of the Government. As I have already said, I think that the new state of affairs is healthier, with Africans bringing their own pressure. And I believe that it should be one of the leading aims of policy everywhere to secure that all sections of public opinion are in a position to do this.

THE COURSE OF CONSTITUTIONAL ADVANCE

The Gold Coast Constitution, 1946

The process of interrelated pressure may be seen recurring right through the political advances from 1946 onwards. I must describe these, starting with West Africa. The first step in constitutional reform after the war, the new Gold Coast constitution of 1946, was designed to meet the political requirements of the time, but was not to any large extent the result of nationalist pressure. Sir Alan Burns succeeded in getting the support of the political leaders, and the new constitution was widely and justly acclaimed as an important advance. It brought Ashanti into the Legislative Council and provided for the election of Ashanti and Colony rural members by the traditional Ashanti Confederacy Council and the Joint Provincial Council of Chiefs. It did not give the Northern Territories representation, but it prepared for this by setting up a Northern Territories Council. It established a very large popular majority in the Legislative Council over officials, and this created the conditions from which further political advance was bound to follow. It gave no new executive responsibility to Africans, leaving the African members of Executive Councils, first appointed during the war, in a purely advisory position without charge of particular spheres of Government activity. Burns laid great stress on the Africanization of the service, informing his officers that anyone who did not believe in this had better get out. At this time also the first two African administrative officers were appointed, Professor Busia (now leader of the Opposition in Ghana) and Mr. Adu (now Permanent Secretary of the Department of External Affairs); it is perhaps surprising that none were appointed before.

The Nigerian Constitution, 1946

The new Nigerian constitution, also of 1946, was more controversial. There had been much criticism by local politicians of the previous state of affairs. But the initiative came mainly from the Governor. In preparing the constitution Sir Arthur Richards consulted the Northern Emirs and some other leading Africans; but the politicians, already strong in the South, felt that he had not sufficiently consulted popular opinion. The scheme came in for a good deal of local attack. But it created the framework of modern Nigeria, and was a great landmark of constitutional advance.

Its main feature was the creation of Regional Councils in the North, West, and East, the North being brought into the central constitutional structure for the first time. The Regional Councils were linked on the one hand with the Native Authorities who elected many of their members, and on the other with the central Legislative Council, which was given an unofficial majority mainly elected by the Regional Councils. These Councils were advisory, but had definite and formal functions with regard to new legislation. The African members of the Executive Council, as in the Gold Coast, were left with advisory functions and were not given executive responsibilities.

The Gold Coast, 1948–1957

No doubt the hopes of further advance which these important constitutional changes aroused and the opportunities they opened up themselves contributed to the growth of nationalist movements. The National Council of Nigeria and the Cameroons was very active in Nigeria during this period, but it was in the Gold Coast that the next great move forward came. The United Gold Coast Convention was founded in 1947 and, when riots took place early in 1948 as a result of ex-servicemen's grievances and popular discontent at rising prices, the party took advantage of this to stir up much political feeling. The Watson Commission, appointed by the Colonial Office to inquire into the causes, stretched and, some said, went outside its terms of reference in recommending radical reform. The British Government thereupon authorized the appointment of an all-African Committee in the Gold Coast, under the late Judge Coussey, to consider a scheme of constitutional advance. From this Committee and subsequent deliberation by the British Government emerged a new constitution, introduced in 1950, with an almost entirely African Legislature, mostly elected indirectly, and a predominantly African Ministry, the Ministers being appointed by the Governor subject to the approval of the Assembly—in fact a system well on the way to responsible government.

While this process of constitution-making was going forward, the Convention People's Party was founded by Dr. Kwame Nkrumah, and, in spite of his being sentenced to prison by the courts when he tried direct action at the end of 1949, the C.P.P. organized itself most efficiently and swept the board in the elections, whereupon Nkrumah emerged from prison to form the first representative government, at Sir Charles

Arden-Clarke's invitation. He became the first Prime Minister in 1952; 1954 saw an all-African Cabinet and a directly elected Legislature, the Governor retaining certain reserve powers. Independence followed in 1957.

This bald recital does not do justice to the remarkable co-operation between the Governor and Prime Minister in carrying the country through these critical years of transition, an achievement that has received the high praise it deserves. Some have criticized the decisions of 1948 and 1949, by which the point of no return was passed, on the ground that the advance was too rapid. The official view at the time was that no constitution which did not give a real share in the Government to the people of the Gold Coast had any chance of succeeding. The change from a largely official form of government to a ministerial system was certainly abrupt and, as things turned out, the educated and professional class of the Gold Coast, from whom the main critics of the old system had been drawn before the C.P.P. was founded, had little part in the new Government. Looking back it may be regretted—although such regrets are futile—that they were not brought in earlier. But the new men who formed the Government in 1950, although most of them did not come from the old professional class, were highly educated men. I well remember the telegram from the Governor giving the names of the new Cabinet. It ended up: "All but Braimah (from the Northern Territories) and myself (a young man in the First World War) are university graduates."

Nigeria, 1948–1958

Nigeria could not be left static while the Gold Coast was advancing rapidly. Accordingly Sir John Macpherson proposed to the Legislative Council in 1948 that a constitutional review should start in the following year. This consisted of consultations at the divisional, provincial, and regional levels, followed by a representative Nigerian Conference in 1950. The constitution which emerged carried on the process started by Richards. A Council of Ministers was set up at the Center, and Regional Executive Councils in the Regions, all with a substantial majority of Nigerians. The Regional Governments and Assemblies were given responsibility for a considerable range of subjects. The Assemblies were indirectly elected except in the West, and a House of Chiefs in the West was added to that already existing in the North. The Central Legislature continued to be elected from the membership of the Regional Assemblies. It covered a wide range of subjects and had residual legislative power, while legislation could not be introduced in the Regional Houses without the approval of the Central Council of Ministers. The constitution was in fact quasi-federal. After the election the two leading politicians in Nigeria, Dr. Azikiwe and Chief Awolowo, entered the Eastern and Western Regional Governments as the principal Ministers. From now on the interaction of pressures for further advance was between the British Government and the different Governments in Nigeria, the complex of forces in Nigeria being a highly elaborate one.

In practice the structure of the constitution turned out to be too closely knit for the three regions to work effectively together. After two representative conferences in 1953 and 1954 between the Secretary of State and the Nigerian leaders, a true federation emerged with an increased range of subjects in the hands of the Regional Governments and Legislatures. These were given residual legislative powers. Regional Premiers were appointed and internal self-government promised for any region which wanted it in 1956; but the Federal Legislature was further enlarged and was now separately elected. After a further similar conference in 1957, the East and West were given self-government in regional affairs and the North will get it in 1959. The Southern Cameroons, part of the Territory under Trusteeship administered with Nigeria, had been separated from the Eastern Region in 1954 and given its own Government; the process was then carried further by establishing an office of Premier and a ministerial system for the Southern Cameroons. Most important of all, an all-Nigerian Federal Ministry was established, and a Nigerian Prime Minister took office late in 1957, the Governor-General retaining certain reserve powers. And it was agreed that for the next elections, late in 1959, a bicameral system should be established for the Federal Legislature with the House of Representatives on a population basis and a Senate in which the Regions and the Southern Cameroons would be equally represented.

This remarkable series of consultations between the Secretary of State, the Governor-General, and Regional Governors and political leaders from all parts of Nigeria has brought this great and varied country to the last stages of constitutional advance. Because the population of the Northern Region is greater than that of the other two regions put together, and in spite of the fact that the North is educationally although not economically a good deal more backward than the others, the governing party in the North is the majority party in the federal scene and the first Prime Minister is a Northerner. This party, the Northern People's Congress, largely represents the established elements, the Emirs and their counselors and officers. Not only in the North but in the West also the Chiefs have played a prominent part in political development and public life. The three main political parties, all primarily tribal, have each dominated one region, the N.C.N.C. the East, which is primarily Ibo, the Action Group the West, primarily Yoruba, and the N.P.C. the North, primarily Hausa-Fulani. The N.C.N.C. has some support among the Yorubas and has provided the opposition in the West, but has not come near to gaining a majority. The Action Group has some support in the East. Although the N.P.C. has a majority in the Federal legislature, no one party can hope to control the whole country at present. Hence, when independence comes, no single party will be able to claim the main credit for this. Although the stresses and strains between the regions are inevitably bound to be great, there seems a good chance of a balance being preserved.

East Africa

Turning to East Africa, there are three controversial subjects which I have no time to do more than mention. The first has to do with the East Africa High Commission, which was set up after the war to provide an executive machine to operate certain services of a non-political type common to the three Territories, such as inter-territorial communications and research; an Assembly was included to legislate for these services and review their working publicly. The High Commission consists of the three Governors; the common services are financed and the unofficial members of the Assembly largely elected by the Territorial Legislatures; no legislation can go forward to the Assembly without the agreement of the three Governments. The High Commission and Assembly in fact work with delegated authority from the Territories; the scheme is thus not a political federation. There have been objections to the High Commission in some parts of East Africa, particularly Buganda; but many people, Africans and others, realize its value and its unpolitical character. The British Government has given a solemn assurance that federation will not be imposed so long as the people of the Territories are opposed to this. Secondly I cannot go into the withdrawal of recognition from the Kabaka of Buganda and his subsequent reinstatement; a judgment on this complicated series of events must be left to political scientists and historians. I shall have something to say later about the relations of Buganda with the rest of Uganda. Finally I do not propose to deal with the Mau Mau uprising in Kenya.

The first step by the East African Governments in the period after 1940 was to introduce African representation in the Legislative Councils. By the end of 1952 there were eight Africans out of sixteen unofficial members in Uganda, six out of twenty-eight in Kenya, and four out of fourteen in Tanganyika. There were two African members of the Governor's Executive Council in Uganda and one in Kenya, in each case, like the other unofficial members, without executive responsibility; earlier two Europeans from public life had joined the Government in Kenya and in fact became virtually officials. The African members of Legislative Councils were nominated, although associated with particular areas, in some cases in Uganda being selected by Provincial Councils. So few members could clearly not effectively represent vast numbers of constituents. But it was the principle of African representation which was important; it was bound to lead to a more fully representative system later.

Tanganyika

The main political pressures in East Africa in the last fifteen years have been in Kenya and Uganda. In Tanganyika political activity was slower to develop. In 1954 in Tanganyika a system of equal representation for Africans, Asians, and Europeans was introduced in the Legislative Council, each race having ten members on the representative side; this is known as parity. At the same time Africans came into the Executive

Council as unofficial members, each of the three races having
two of these. Last year six Assistant Ministers were appointed,
four of them Africans, and it was made clear that this was in
preparation for the appointment of full Ministers at a later
stage. In 1958 and 1959 elections to the Legislative Council
are being held in Tanganyika on a common roll for the first
time in East Africa, but with a reservation of seats which main-
tains the parity principle.

All these measures were taken on the initiative of the Governor, Sir Edward Twining, but political pressure has recently
begun to make itself felt. The constitution has been criticized
by the nationalist party, the Tanganyika African National
Union, which has claimed that parity in the Legislature is unfair to Africans because of their great preponderance of numbers, and objects to the obligation laid on voters in contested
elections to vote for candidates of all three races or spoil their
ballots. But T.A.N.U. has announced that it will contest the
elections. The Governor has stated that, when they are over
in 1959, a Committee with representatives of the new Legislature will be set up to consider further constitutional reforms,
including the question whether parity should be retained. The
Tanganyika Government has held the initiative so far, but will
have to reckon with steadily increasing political pressure in the
future.

Uganda

In Uganda the Legislative Council was substantially enlarged in 1953, with the object among other things of linking
each district with the center through the election of an African
member by its District Council; Buganda was to have three
members. There had been some requests for such an arrange-

ment in some Districts, but there was no political pressure for it. The Buganda Lukiko's refusal to elect members was one of the elements in the Buganda constitutional crisis of 1953. It was only as part of the settlement by which the Kabaka was reinstated in 1955 that Buganda was persuaded to send members to the Legislative Council, after it had been agreed that the number should be increased to five and that half the members of the Legislative Council and three-fifths of the representative side should be Africans. Another element in this constitutional scheme was the setting up of a ministerial system for Uganda as a whole, with six official Ministers and five drawn from the public (three Africans, a European, and an Asian).

In the negotiations in London leading up to this settlement the Baganda representatives, no doubt responding at that time to nationalist pressures, urged that direct elections should be introduced; but they eventually accepted the indirect method for the elections immediately to follow, with a review of the system promised in 1957. In 1956 I announced that the Government would work for direct elections throughout the country in 1961, on a common roll, with safeguards to secure effective representation for minorities and with experimental direct elections for Africans in Buganda in 1957 and indirect elections elsewhere in that year. The nationalist party, the Uganda National Congress, which had been active since 1953 and particularly so during the Buganda crisis, rejected my proposals, though in somewhat half-hearted terms. But the pressure from other districts was stronger; while supporting the plan generally they strongly objected to the special treatment of Buganda. They refused to respond to arguments advanced by the Government to drop this objection, and later, very wisely I think, my successor, Sir Frederick Crawford, agreed to direct elections in any district which wants it. After a great deal of negotiation the Buganda Lukiko was persuaded to accept a franchise which was very wide but not universal—bringing in among others all owners and tenants of land. The preparations for elections throughout the country then went forward. After the arrangements for registration had actually started, a *volte face* occurred in Buganda. The traditionalists around the Buganda Government apparently turned against the political parties and the Lukiko decided that it did not want direct elections. The whole story is instructive as showing the interplay of pressures between traditionalists and nationalists.

Kenya

In Kenya the story is equally interesting. In 1954 the Secretary of State (then Mr. Lyttelton) succeeded in persuading local opinion to accept a ministerial government containing members of all races, with six official Ministers, two nominated Ministers (the two who had joined the Government earlier), and six Ministers drawn from the public (three Europeans, two Asians and an African). As part of the settlement it was agreed that there should be no change before 1960 unless the representatives of all races agreed or the constitution became unworkable; each race thus had a veto on change. Early in 1957 elections took place for the African representative seats, which had been increased from six to eight by agreement between the races; the franchise was wider than that for Tanganyika but narrower than that for Uganda. The men elected were fairly advanced nationalists and, under the leadership of Mr. Tom Mboya, immediately announced that they would not take part in the Government (in which a second African Minister had already been promised); they also asked for fifteen more African seats on the Legislative Council.

The next development is of great interest. The European members after due deliberation announced that they might be prepared to consider *some* increase in African representation without compensation on their side, provided that the Africans agreed to take part in the Government and some arrangement could be made to safeguard the future position of Europeans in Kenya. In spite of all the efforts of the Secretary of State, Mr. Lennox-Boyd, both in London and in Kenya, no agreement could be reached, the African members refusing to negotiate unless their demand for fifteen new seats on the Legislature were first met. At this point the European and Asian members of the Government resigned and the Secretary of State was thus free to take action; in fact he imposed the settlement which then came into force.

The main points in it were six more communal seats for Africans, bringing their numbers on the representative side of Legislative Council up to the European numbers; the creation of twelve special seats, four for each race, to be elected by all the members of Legislative Council, including the officials, voting together; and a statement that there would be no more communal seats in future changes. Finally the Secretary of State decided to establish a Council of State for Kenya to protect each race from discriminatory legislation. The Council will have power to delay legislation, comment on it to the Legislative Council, or ask for it to be reserved for examination by the British Government. It will consist of a chairman and ten members appointed by the Governor from all races, but not chosen as racial representatives. The settlement has been rejected by the African members of Legislative Council; but in spite of their disapproval Africans have come forward as candidates for the special seats. The elections for the six new African communal seats have produced some members at any rate in sympathy with the existing African members. It is too early to say what will happen.

The new arrangement shows the shift of emphasis which has occurred recently in Kenya politics. The fact that (unlike the

African Affairs Board in the Central African Federation) the Council of State is designed to protect not only African interests but those of all races shows the political pressure which Africans can now bring to bear in Kenya and are expected to be able to bring to bear in the future. The Europeans, traditionally intolerant of control by Whitehall as other British colonists had been before them, are now beginning to look to the British Government to support their interests. Their position should be understood. They went to Kenya in good faith; indeed they were encouraged to do so by the Governments of the day. They have made it their home, built up its wealth, and to a very large extent are responsible for its development. They are pioneers like the pioneers of the Western United States. Their contribution is very important to the future progress of the country, including the advancement of Africans. They have the right to expect to have their interests safeguarded by Government. And Government must do this while at the same time continuing its traditional function of promoting the well-being and advancement of Africans. There are signs that increasing numbers of Europeans recognize that ultimately their future depends on the special contribution they can go on making as individuals to the progress of the country and on Africans realizing the value of that special contribution. Broadly speaking the same applies to Asians both in Kenya and elsewhere in East Africa.

NATIONALISM AND TRIBAL LOYALTY

Race Problems

Racial conflict and adjustment is apt to be regarded as the dominant political issue in Africa. In both West and East

African Territories, nationalist movements are racial in the
sense that they are movements by Africans for independence
from European control. They are not, however, race struggles
in the classic sense between competing sections of a settled
population such as we see at the northern and southern ends of
Africa. In the Territories we are considering there are no large
settlements of Europeans except in Kenya, with small groups
in Tanganyika and with Asians settled throughout East Africa.
These settled communities are very small in numbers compared to the whole population and there are already signs
that they are adjusting themselves to this fact. In West Africa
the nationalist movement has been directed not at other groups
in the population but at colonial Government as such. When
Africans got political power in West Africa, or felt sure
they were going to get it, the racial aspect of nationalism
to a large extent fell away. Europeans generally speaking are
popular in Ghana, just as they are in India. While therefore
no one would deny the importance of racial problems, it may
turn out that problems of adjustment between the tribe and the
nation are even more important.

The Effects of Tribalism

In the part of Africa I know best, nationalism so far is less
powerful than tribalism, and this is natural, since it is a recent
growth, whereas tribalism is deeply rooted in custom and
tradition. Tribalism may be a force making for progress,
as it has been among the Chagga in northern Tanganyika,
where the economic prosperity derived from coffee growing
and a successful cooperative movement have brought an up-
surge of tribal pride and great advances in education, trading,
and development generally. Much of the work of economic and

social advance in British Territories has, indeed, been done through the tribe. But, on the other hand, opposition to Government measures, whether the Government be composed of overseas officials or elected Ministers, may take the form of a reversion to tribalism. Traditional elements in African society—Chiefs, elders and all others who want to preserve the status quo—may rely on this tribal feeling, which may be a valuable force of restraint in periods of rapid transition, but may be the focus for reaction or opposition to Government. I am not talking here of violent opposition, the most abnormal and extreme case of which was the Mau Mau outbreak, a reversion to tribalism in a perverted and brutal form. I am talking of opposition by orderly means, as for example by a Native Authority to this or that measure proposed by the Central Government, something which is a normal and understandable part of the process of adjusting to modern ideas.

The Tribe in Nation-Building

It is sometimes assumed that British policy in Africa is based on the principle of divide and rule. This is not correct. The policy is, rather, unite and let them rule. In all these countries our aim in recent years has been to build a nation out of a collection of tribes. In the process of building the British administration has been the steel scaffolding which has held each country together; that is why stresses and strains tend to appear when the British go or show signs of preparing to go. It is sometimes asked why we concentrate on the building up of countries with artificial boundaries and different ethnic groups, with many languages, sometimes as different in the same country as English is from Arabic; Tanganyika for example, with its 8½ million people, has over a hundred separate languages. The reason is that collections of tribes, each with their own administration, could not provide the services which the people need and demand, and would not be strong enough to stand on their own feet as viable states in the modern world. For these purposes strong Central Governments are needed, whatever constitutional form they may take.

Tribalism nevertheless is a great complicating element in the process of nation-building. Difficulties between the traditional elements of the Ashanti tribe and the Central Government started soon after the ministerial system was set up in the Gold Coast and have persisted since. They were probably due in part to the fact that Ashanti came into the central political system of the Gold Coast only some four years before the constitutional changes of 1950. I have already referred to the relations between the great tribal groups which dominate the three regions of Nigeria. Here problems arise between smaller tribal groups and the Regional Governments. There have been movements for setting up more regions; in the West from Benin and neighboring areas; in the East from the Ibibio and the Efiks; in the North from the Middle Belt. Such breaking up of the regions would further complicate the federal structure and would create great difficulties in finance, administration, and manpower. But by agreement of the last representative conference on Nigeria in 1957, the matter is being investigated by a high-powered outside Commission, which has been enjoined to see whether there are other ways of satisfying the fears of these minority groups; and it is only if no such other ways are found that the Commission is entitled to suggest the creation of new regions.

Tribal Problems in Uganda

In Uganda tribal feeling has appeared in its most pronounced form; this is probably due to the relative position and strength of Buganda when compared with the rest of the country. Buganda is larger in population than the other tribal areas; is richer; has more education; through its earlier contact with Europeans is generally more advanced; is situated at the center of the country; has the main governmental centers of the country in it; and has a more elaborate system of government with more powers and services under its control. Moreover, tribal pride, which has its roots in the superior development of the Baganda before the arrival of the British, is very strong and widespread. Many Baganda fear that the rest of the country might hold their progress back, and this was part of the reason which prompted them to come out in favor of separation from the rest and a separate move to independence, a demand which was at the root of the 1953 crisis. Looking further ahead many Baganda would like to be the dominant force in an independent Uganda. The other tribes both envy the Baganda their institutions and their progress and fear domination by them.

What was our policy in this situation? It was twofold. On the one hand we strove to build up the central institutions of the country, the central Executive and Legislature; to increase the number of Africans in both these bodies and in the higher civil service; to link each part of the country with the center through representation in the Legislature and other bodies; and to introduce direct elections to the Legislative Council. On the other hand we tried to develop the political and social institutions of each part of the country, in Buganda by giving the Lukiko an elected majority and the Buganda Government a ministerial system of its own and responsibility for the running of education, health, and agricultural and veterinary services at the provincial level, and in the rest of the country by increasing the elected element in the District Councils and giving them responsibility for local services in their areas, primary education, rural water supplies, etc.

This policy has been criticized on the ground that it was inconsistent to devolve power to Buganda and the other areas at the same time as we were seeking to build up the center. It has been argued that by so doing we strengthened parochial feelings among the different tribes and weakened the unity of the country. There is, of course, room for two views on this, but I think that the criticism misses the point. Strong tribal feeling existed before the reforms of recent years, and the Buganda Government has been highly organized and treated in a special way for over fifty years. Political advance was bound to bring out the strength of tribal loyalties, with the Protectorate Government regarded as an outside Government however benevolent and the Buganda Government and the other Native Governments and Authorities as the people's own Governments. Not to have recognized this state of affairs would have been harmful or at the least unreal, and the view we took was that strengthening the unity of the country would not be furthered by failing to recognize the attachment of the people to the parts.

It was for this reason that we thought it right to give each of them definite functions to perform, not only in law and order and finance, but also in social and economic development. Of course the greater powers given to the Native Governments and Authorities in the different areas, and the greater element of popular representation, have created difficulties for the Central Government; that was inevitable. When political advances are made either at the center or in local affairs, one must not be dismayed when people use their new powers in their own way. Constitutional advance is not a puppet show. A sense of responsibility can only be acquired by exercising responsibility. And in the end, when the constitution of the country has finally to be worked out, the fact that tribal loyalties have been institutionalized may prove a strength, not a weakness.

At the present time what the London *Times* correspondent in Kampala calls neo-traditionalism is strong in Buganda; it was, of course, strengthened by the deposition and reinstatement of the Kabaka. But not all Baganda, to say nothing of others, take the traditionalist view. A considerable number of people understand the value of a united Uganda; these views are not popular, but they are sometimes expressed publicly. And there are other forces at work in Buganda and elsewhere, forces which are bound to grow stronger in time. These include the broadening influence of education, particularly higher education at Makerere College; the steady growth of a propertied middle class in trade, the cooperative movement, and the professions; the growth of national political parties, not only the Uganda National Congress but the Democratic Party. Although the politically minded have sometimes expressed separatist views in reaction against the Government insistence on unity, in the long run it is difficult to see how they could be in favor of a fragmented country.

THE NATIONALIST

Some people see a nationalist as either a hero or a dangerous fanatic. He may of course be either, as anyone else may. But this is not the correct image. I have written earlier of some of the causes which produce nationalism. We must remember also the difficulties which a nationalist has to face. He has to bridge the gulf between his home, often in the village, and the British university he attended. He has to work with people who are often uneducated and know nothing of the outside world; with his education and knowledge, he is thereby subjected to great temptation, because many of those he talks to will have no standard by which to judge much of what he tells them. He nearly always carries a slight, or a fancied slight, by Europeans in Africa, Europe, or indeed North America. But in spite of this he is usually friendly to individual Europeans, and is almost always deeply attached to the ultimate goals of the West. He is distressed by the great gap between the existing state of affairs in his country, with all its physical and human limitations on rapid advance, and his own ideal for it as he would like to see it, with self-government, a respected culture, and a modern economic apparatus. He feels emotionally that with independence he and his fellows will be able to bridge this gap, but he knows in his mind that this will be a hard, long, and difficult task and that help from outside experts of all kinds will be needed for a very long time even after independence.

What should our attitude towards nationalists be? First, and above all, we should treat them neither as saints nor as agitators, but as individuals with whom we should make every effort to establish human contact. Secondly, we should not be disappointed when a nationalist turns out to be less than perfect. We tend to hold nationalists to utopian standards. We should recognize that as people they are not essentially different from the rest of us, although their societies as they are now may expose them to different, and often greater, temptations. Thirdly, we should realize that it is the business of nationalists to oppose colonial Governments, because they aim at putting an end to the colonial system of government. If they are subversive or go in for violence, as they sometimes do, this must be firmly resisted and dealt with; for nationalists are not above the law. But just because they oppose Governments we should not confuse nationalism with communism. Nationalists may, of course, make contacts with communists, although until now they have done so in Africa only to a limited extent. But if we confuse nationalism with communism, we are doing a most harmful thing, because successful cooperation with nationalism is our greatest bulwark against communism in Africa.

Fourthly, we should realize that nationalists provide some of the dynamic force in societies which in Africa are often static or inert, and that, in their social, educational, and economic ideas and as unifying forces, the aims of these nationalists are often largely the same as our own, the main difference being in the pace of advance which they wish to see. Fifthly, we should be cautious about describing a nationalist party as non-representative just because it is relatively small in numbers. In the African countries we are considering nationalist movements are bound to grow steadily more powerful as increased numbers of educated leaders come forward and as the people gain in economic strength and can thus bring more and more pressure in politics. The intelligent thing is for Governments to recognize this early and by skillful anticipation to try to guide the energies of nationalists into constructive channels and to secure their cooperation in a program of steady but not head-long political advance. Of course where there is a failure of cooperation between the Government and a national party, the fault may well be and frequently is that of the nationalists more than that of the Government.

Sixthly, we should realize that successful working with nationalists is the smoothest way of helping a country to self-government. Of course the nationalists are not the only people we have to work with. At all stages of political advance we have the duty of safeguarding and helping forward the more backward sections of the African population. In the later stages we have the duty of safeguarding minority racial communities. This latter task in particular may complicate our dealings with the nationalists. It is something nevertheless which we must tackle; in doing so we must seek to persuade the nationalists that the safeguarding of minorities is an essential part of the process of political advance, while much will, of course, depend on the attitude of the minority groups themselves to African aspirations. Finally, we should remember that when countries become independent they are bound to act in an independent way and, if sometimes they do things which we do not like, we should not hold up our hands in pious horror as if all were lost. Rather we should look back at the history of our own countries. We might read *The Reason Why*, which tells how the British Army was run at the time of the Crimean War, or we might reflect that even in the most advanced countries public life is not always perfect.

THREE

The Tasks of Government

THIS TALK is devoted to British officers and the part they have played. I have spoken of nationalism as a dynamic force in Africa, but our own policy has been an influence of far longer standing in the process of transforming society in Africa—and British officers have been the spearheads of progress. The Governments of the Territories, supported by missionary effort and private enterprise, have spread education and medical services, extended communications, provided water supplies, introduced cash crops, improved cattle-keeping, forestry and fisheries, developed trade, and so on. All over these countries British officers—administrators, doctors, educators, agriculturists, engineers, and many others—with the Chiefs with whom they have worked, have been the leaders of the people. They led them at first by paternalistic means, later with the people themselves playing a continually increasing part. In West Africa many Africans are now working alongside British officers in the senior levels of the Government services. In East Africa the same process has started. But, even with the great political advances which have taken place recently, British officers are still supplying a very large part of the dynamic force.

However important policy and policy-making may be, human relations are still more important in successful government and development. Above all is this so in Africa, where the processes of government and public life are still relatively uncomplicated by Western standards, and where much of the work is carried on between people of different race, language, and background. With Africans it is the man and his personality which count.

The main contact between the Government and the people is at the district level or below it, as well as in the towns; district administration is thus the foundation of Government. In most British Territories several districts are grouped together into a province. The Provincial Commissioner directs the district staffs, guiding them, stimulating them, and acting as the link between them and the Central Government. The Provincial Commissioner, in intimate touch with his District Commissioners, is a key figure in the government machine. But I am going to talk mainly about the men who work in districts, whether as administrators or technical officers. I am not, of course, unmindful of the great part played by many other people—Borup introducing cotton to Uganda when working for the Church Missionary Society; Swynnerton organizing the attack on the tsetse fly in East Africa; and Bennett helping the Chagga to build up the Kilimanjaro Native Cooperative Union and the coffee industry which is the foundation of their wealth. Nor do I forget the pioneers of trade, mining, and industry.

THE BRITISH OFFICER IN THE FIELD

A District Commissioner and his staff are responsible for very many things. They must supervise the courts and native administration in all its forms; build up local government; safeguard African land rights; and help the technical officers in the district in their dealings with the African Authorities. They are closely involved in local development and education, since the D.C. is often the chairman of the Local Education Authority; they administer the towns and deal with the affairs of the commercial community; they have a great variety of routine functions, such as licensing and making returns, all of which take up a vast amount of time. In the old days administrative officers did much practical work in the field, such as building roads and making dams; and in some territories they still do these things. Above all the D.C. is responsible for keeping law and order, and he is expected to do so without the use of force except in the last resort. The story is told of a young British officer who during the women's anti-tax riots at Aba in Eastern Nigeria during the 1920's calmed a great and menacing crowd of angry women by talking to them and turning the laugh against an old woman in the front. Laughter resolves many situations in Africa, as I know from my own experience.

District Work in Uganda

I should like to illustrate the work of district staffs from one or two districts in Uganda at different stages of development. Let no one think that I am starting with less advanced districts because they are less advanced; they present a problem for the country, both now and in the future, and they well illustrate the great practical contribution which British officers are making. First of all I will discuss the most backward district in Uganda, Karamoja, which is not at all typical of the rest of the country. The Karamojong and Suk are scattered and semi-nomadic cattle-keepers, practicing little farming and living largely off their cattle. They are only starting education; a few children are rather grudgingly produced for inspection at their meetings with Government officers. At one of the primary mission schools I visited the oldest pupil was 42. The Karamojong and Suk raid each other for cattle and often kill people in the process. The Chiefs here are not strong and often fail to assert themselves with the people. It is the D.C. and his staff, traveling the countryside in Land Rovers with the police and the African government agents, who keep the peace and lay down the law.

But an even more difficult and vital task is saving the land. One can see what the land is like from any of the mountains which rise sheer from the great plains of this district. I had my last view of these a few days before I left Africa, when my wife and I climbed Debasian, a 10,000 foot mountain in southern Karamoja—she is said to have been the first woman ever to have gone to the top. All around us, but particularly to the north and east, stretched vast expanses of barren country with little water. By overgrazing of cattle much of this country has been brought somewhere near ruin. The task of arresting the process is formidable. With scientific study and careful planning, rehabilitation is starting slowly and painfully to be put in hand. A special team is working with the district staff for this purpose. The people are being encouraged to sell their surplus cattle in markets run by the Government. By the building of reservoirs in strategic places they are being encouraged to move to less crowded parts of the district. Much against their will areas are being set aside to rest the exhausted grazing. The tsetse fly has been eliminated from a great area which it had invaded and, by cutting down and keeping down the trees on a wide strip drawn between two ranges of mountains, a barrier has been placed like a cork in a bottle against the return of the fly from over the northern frontier with the Sudan. Field officers are living at isolated points in the district to carry out all this work.

In fact in Karamoja the initiative comes almost entirely from the British officers. It is an uphill task, for the people are intensely resistant to change and inclined to violence if pressed too far. A year or so before I left Uganda I visited the Karasuk and held a meeting with them. The men were sitting in a half circle under a tree, resplendent with their ostrich plumes; their spears according to practice had been safely stacked a hundred yards away. Behind them at a little distance stood the women in all their finery. Speaking through double interpretation I told them all the things they must do—sell their cattle, send their children to school (none of them popular things)—and all the things they must not do, things which they wanted to do, such as raiding the Karamojong and grazing their cattle on closed areas. They were angry because one such area, a large one, had been set aside for resting and to create a no man's land between them and the Karamojong. A spokesman with a lion's mane as headdress and a tin ornament hanging from his nose stood up to speak. He said: "You are the Head of this country. No Governor has ever been to this place before and you have done us a great honor by coming. This is a great day. But what use is it to us because you have simply told us all the things which the District Commissioner had told us before?" There was much murmuring and signs of the women bubbling over. Not long afterwards the District Commissioner asked me to bring the meeting to an end. This whole area is a relic of the past; it brings home to one graphically the vital pioneering work of British officers at an earlier period.

Let us turn to a very different district, Kigezi in Southwest Uganda. Here the people are much more advanced, living in a different world. There are able Chiefs under a Secretary-General, strong and effective leaders. There is an elected District Council and a functioning local government machine. Education has been extended widely. In this mountainous area with its hard-working people the problem is overpopulation. Let us look from any hilltop into one of the narrow valleys of the district. What does one see? First of all the steep hillsides terraced for cultivation, an anti-erosion measure patiently pressed on the people by Agricultural Officers and Chiefs and now everywhere adopted; black wattle plantations on the slopes; a road recently built by community effort winding round the hillside; and huts everywhere in close clusters, with many signs of improved housing as a result of campaigns by the Health Inspector. There is hardly a square yard of unfarmed land to be seen, either in the valley or on the slopes or on the hilltops. Only the swamp at the bottom of the valley is empty and this is gradually being drained and used for food crops. An expert brought by the Government has taught the people to build fishponds and many of these are to be seen in the valley. In short, all the Government officers working in the district and all the Chiefs are engaged in a concerted campaign to safeguard the land with all means in their power.

The only real solution here is more efficient farming. The District Agricultural Officer and his trained African staff have done an agricultural survey of the whole district, and, with the aid of the Chiefs, Field Officers posted in different places are teaching the people to improve their methods. Considerable numbers of people have been persuaded to settle in less crowded areas both inside and outside Kigezi. The district has a long struggle against overpopulation in front of it. The task of Government officers is clear and hard, to lead the Chiefs and the people in tackling this problem.

The neighboring district of Ankole has an efficient Native Government under its ruler, the Omugabe, with a chief executive called the Enganzi or Prime Minister; the two Enganzis I knew during my time were highly educated, modern, and progressive administrators. The development of the district went forward by a process of fruitful cooperation between them and the D.C. and other Government officers. Here the most important task is to improve the cattle economy. Again, there was an intensive campaign to stamp out the tsetse fly, this time by cutting down all the high acacia trees over a wide area, but leaving other trees standing—what is known as discriminative clearing. I well remember the scientific officer in charge explaining the scheme to one of the local leaders with a large-scale map showing every tree. The local leader said, "If you cut down those trees the fly will go into others." But he was wrong. The scheme has gone forward and the fly has been eliminated from this part of the district. The cattle have immense horns and are loved by the people. The Omugabe once admitted to me that these horns were uneconomic, but he said, "They are so beautiful." The District Veterinary Officer is a key man. The one I particularly knew won the confidence of the people, even if he was only beginning to persuade them that cattle are an economic asset, not simply something which brings prestige to their owners. He was so effective that some of them even lent him some of their own young stock to demonstrate to these conservative people the value of raising calves at range instead of in stall.

I wish I could speak of other districts, such as Bunyoro, where the District Commissioner, through the good relations he had with both sides, was mainly responsible for a successful negotiation for the grant of a constitution between the Ruler and a group of educated and professional men among his subjects; or Bugisu on the slopes of Mount Elgon, with its remarkable African Secretary-General, its often difficult cooperative union, and its valuable coffee industry which produced money to finance many schemes of local improvement. Roads were driven into inaccessible valleys high up the slopes of the mountain to develop the coffee industry, housing was improved, schools built, water supplies provided. In all these things the

British officers and the Secretary-General worked closely together.

Bugisu, like some other districts, was more affected by politics than the other districts I have talked about. The D.C. was often heavily involved in them, particularly where the local branch of the nationalist political party campaigned mainly about local grievances and against the Chiefs, as such branches often do. The D.C. had the delicate task of holding the ring between different factions and seeing that the authority of the Chiefs was not improperly attacked; sometimes he had to take action to keep the peace.

Local Government Work

In talking about district administration, I have not said enough yet about local government work; it is certainly the most important part of what a D.C. has to do. What does it consist of? Advising and guiding the Senior Officers of the local African Authority over their finances, their building programs, their staff problems, and many other things. Discussing with them new plans or proposals—the setting up of a new committee of the District Council, the introduction of elections, the taking over from the Central Government of another local service. Discussing these things also, or explaining Government policy or plans to the General Purposes Committee of the Council, or to the Council itself, listening to the comments of members, answering their questions, spending hours in the process of explanation and even vigorous argument in bodies where strong views are held and freely expressed. Helping and guiding country and lower Chiefs throughout the District, meeting lower councils and village gatherings, discussing their local affairs and explaining Government policy and District plans to them. It is a continuous process of educating the local officials, leaders, and people in the art of democratic local government—no easy process of adjustment to new ideas and new methods—a process demanding in the British officers working in the districts a combination of patient diplomacy and firm leadership, together with a willingness to let others learn by experience, sometimes painful, to do what the British officer himself could do more quickly and more easily. It is in fact the process which we have insisted on, of training Africans in responsibility in each area of the country.

I will not speak now of the complicated affairs of Buganda. Here the administrative officers of the Central Government are in a different position from other parts of the country, and there is no district administration. The task of the Resident and his staff under the Buganda Agreement is to advise and help the Kabaka's Government and its officers. The work in fact is largely diplomatic, although the Central Government under the Agreement has over-all responsibility, through its relationship with the Kabaka's Government, for the well-being and progress of Buganda.

A District Commissioner's Task

The task of the administrative officer in the ordinary district contains four elements: leadership, coordination, diplomacy, and continuity. The progress of the district depends, perhaps more than anything, on the D.C.'s power as a leader, for he must supply the initiative and to a large extent the ideas and plans for the future. It is his task, in fact, to see to it that the policies and programs of the Central Government are carried into effect in the field. In this he must work with all the departmental officers in the district and insure that their work is coordinated, since nothing is worse in dealing with an African peasantry than conflicting injunctions from different departments—something not completely unknown in the past. Excessive numbers of new schemes all operating at the same time, however good in themselves, will confuse the people and defeat their own object. To avoid such confusion Uganda adopted the system of district teams, in which the D.C. and all the technical officers in the district work together with the heads of the African Local Authority. They are matched by provincial teams of officers working at the provincial level. The same thing has been done in several other Territories. District teams are concerned primarily with economic and social development; they produce district plans as a framework for coordinated action. But it is recognized that these plans, like all other Government programs, cannot be forced on the people. If they are to be effective the people must be persuaded to accept them, and the process of persuasion may take weeks or even months. It is a process which cannot either be rushed or avoided; nothing is more important in district administration. But if an officer is to be effective he must be known to the people he works with; hence the vital importance of continuity of service in a single area. Often, through shortage of staff and the consequent absence of spare men to fill gaps, this continuity has not been kept up and the public interest has suffered. I made it a rule in Uganda that no D.C. should be moved within five years without my personal authority. As one of the Rulers once said to me, this is a good rule—provided you like the D.C.

The British Officer and the People

The criticism has been made that British officers are in less close personal touch than they used to be with the people of the district. There is some truth in this, but only some. In the old days when many officers did not marry until a good deal later than now, and when the business of government was simpler than it is today, more time could be spent touring round the district, and the tours were more leisurely since much of them was done on foot. Moreover, the simplicity of the work itself made for a closer relationship with Chiefs and other Africans. All the technological advances which have since taken place and the growing complexity of government have tended to make contacts rather more difficult than they once were. Perhaps too much emphasis has been placed on the system, on order and method in administration, necessary though those things are. I remember being struck when I visited a native administration in Northern Nigeria at being shown the great account books almost as if they were religious emblems and the be all and end all of life.

In more recent years the presence of wives and children with officers, the great increase in routine business, the work generated by new plans and policies in every field of government activity, the increase for that very reason in the European population of the districts, both official and private—some of them people more interested in their specializd work than in relationships with Africans, but all of them adding to the responsibilities of the D.C.—all these things have tended to keep him and his officers at headquarters. None the less all administrative officers do tour frequently and are in close touch with Chiefs, councilors, and many other people both on tour and at headquarters. Because they go largely by car, they cover more ground in a shorter space of time. No one who sees them in action could fail to be impressed by the close working together of administrative officers, Chiefs, and local government staff in the process of administering and developing the districts.

Some people may believe that the typical British officer is stiff and formal, a man who dines in his tuxedo even when he is camping in the bush; or at any rate, even if he does not, thinks and behaves as if he did. There may have been some element of truth in this in the past; but I have never seen a tuxedo in the bush and scarcely ever even in district headquarters. The D.C. lives a quite simple life and does not usually give himself airs. Yet some compensations are needed for the restricted and rather petty life of a small up-country station, or even of a larger colonial town. This partly takes the form of British tribal ceremonies, such as Caledonian gatherings and the like, Scottish dancing, and various forms of sport practiced by the British. They are the lifelines of the British abroad to their life and habits back home. And this, of course, to a large extent explains why clubs in these places continue to be exclusive, though there are admittedly other less creditable reasons for this, and it is obviously of great importance that everything possible should be done to build up social contacts between races, as is in fact now being done in Uganda. But, as one who has always done my best to break down racial barriers, I should like to explain that after a long day's work people overseas want to relax in an atmosphere as far as possible reproducing what it is like at home in Britain. I myself very well remember this feeling when I was serving abroad as a young man.

The British Officer and Political Advance

Another criticism sometimes made is that a number of officers, whether administrative or technical, are not in sympathy with the rapid political advance which has taken place in recent years. I believe this criticism to be exaggerated by outside observers of our service, but there is some truth in it. Those who do have these feelings are almost always not opposed to the fact of political advance; they are concerned about its speed. Some take the view that efficiency is everything, perhaps not sufficiently appreciating the fact that training in responsibility is still more important, and that you cannot learn to play the violin except by playing it. There are some also who look back with nostalgia to the days when a D.C. worked by giving direct orders. Some, but only a small number, fail to see that the transfer of power to local people is the culmination of all that we have been trying to do. Some prefer the old-fashioned Chief and the unsophisticated peasant to the modern highly educated professional man or politician. When Dr. Arthur Lewis started his speech at one of the Cambridge conferences of administrative officers over which I was presiding with the remark, "I am the type of person you most dislike, the educated native," he was no doubt partly joking, and in any case his remark could only justly have been addressed to a small part of the audience. For I do not believe that more than a few administrative officers take this particular view.

There may be some truth in what a very wise and liberal administrative officer said to me once, that an officer's service should not be too long because, however progressive he is, he will find it difficult to adjust himself to the political changes which are continually taking place. But the proof of the pudding is in the eating, and what has impressed me more than most things in the period I have known Africa is precisely the great adjustment which many officers, administrative and technical, have made. In the span of their service they have passed from a time when administration was inevitably carried on in a completely paternalistic way, through successive stages of advance to one in which they are working under African Ministers. This has happened not only in West Africa but also now in the Central Government in Uganda. In Buganda also a number of British officers have been seconded, with their consent, to the service of the Kabaka's Government and are working there under African Ministers. These adjustments are naturally not always easy. That they have been and are still being successfully made is a remarkable tribute to the flexibility and resourcefulness of British officers.

In helping Africans prepare for the future, British officers are in fact working themselves out of a job. This they do with admirable cheerfulness. But there is no denying the anxiety over their own future which many of them naturally feel, particularly the younger ones in West Africa. To meet this the Overseas Civil Service was formed and certain guarantees have been given to British officers in Nigeria. Also when the stage of responsible government is reached in a Territory, British officers are given the choice of retiring on compensation terms— a fair and necessary arrangement and one which was also followed in India and elsewhere. Compensation terms sometimes put an officer in a dilemma. He would like to stay, but as a young man with a family cannot afford to refuse the compensation offered him. Many who go do so for this reason, not because they do not like working under an African Government. It is interesting that the Ghana Government, to encourage British officers to stay, has recently offered them re-employment on contract without loss of compensation.

One final point about British officers. Perhaps the most striking characteristic about them as a class is their concern for the people they are working for and with. Most of them not only work very hard, but identify themselves very closely, often parochially, with the people of their area. In Nigeria at one time—perhaps still—if one talked about a Northerner or an Easterner or a Westerner one did not necessarily mean a Hausa, and Ibo, or a Yoruba. One might equally well mean a member of the Northern, Eastern, or Western part of the service. They care tremendously about what they are doing. That is why so often when they leave an area they are remembered with deep affection by the people.

The District Officer and the Central Government

Before I turn from officers in the field to Governors, something should be said about the relations with the Central Governments of district and provincial staffs and field officers generally. In the early days D.C.'s had a large degree of independence. Slow communications, unsettled local conditions, and the spirit of the time all contributed to this. By the inter-war period the administrative system had become more elaborate, and D.C.'s operated on a fairly tight rein in all matters susceptible of central instructions. In the day-to-day running of district affairs, including indirect rule, they enjoyed, and still enjoy, a considerable degree of freedom of action within the policy laid down. They could make their views felt at headquarters through the periodical Provincial Commissioners' Conferences and through the senior officer who represented the provincial administration at headquarters; more recently the growth of African Affairs branches in the Central Governments has helped in this process. Nevertheless there was a good deal of grumbling, as there still is, when the Central Government was held to be paying too little attention to their views. In those days there was only a limited interchange between secretariat and district staffs, and the secretariat officer *pur sang* was regarded with some suspicion in the field, not always justly. In practice the degree of weight carried by the provincial administration in the councils of government depended as it still does on the attitude of the Governor; some Governors kept in close personal touch with the administration in the field.

After the Second World War the growth of Government work of all sorts tended both to increase the volume of instructions sent to D.C.'s and, as I have said, to tie them to their desks to the detriment of the real work of administration and contacts with the people in which they had relative freedom of action. The steadily increasing size of Central Governments, and in particular the setting up of Ministries, put still further burdens on the district staff—burdens which in some Territories were met, at any rate to some extent, by providing them with some degree of secretarial and office assistance. The importance of this had been emphasized by the Colonial Office in a circular of 1947 on local government, which also urged that greater freedom of action should be given to district staffs within a generally accepted policy. Similarly in a circular of 1948 on community development, Governments were urged to make grants for this purpose to provinces or districts, so that administrative and technical officers might have greater freedom to promote schemes of economic and social betterment in their areas. Effect was given to this in Uganda by fixing block grants to each district over a period of five years. Each district team was entitled, subject only to the approval of the provincial team, to choose the projects on which this money should be spent, after due consultation with local opinion in each area. The system, not popular with financial officers, seems to me important if local initiative in field staffs is to be encouraged.

THE GOVERNOR AND THE CENTRAL GOVERNMENT

In colonial administration the Governor has always been the vital figure, and continues to be so until the stage is reached when he hands over power to elected Ministers. The Governor occupies the key position between the field administration, the local Legislature, and the Secretary of State and the Colonial Office. As the Queen's Representative he has a great ceremonial position, symbolized by his silver-braided uniform and his plumed hat. At all important functions in the Territory he occupies the center of the stage. He presides over the Executive Council and, until the constitution has advanced a considerable way, over the Legislative Council also. It is he who holds discussions on important matters with members of the Legislative Council whether in groups or as individuals. Visiting businessmen and industrialists often make contact with him personally. Local people of many kinds go to him when they have grievances against the Government. If he unbends even on informal occasions the pompous tend to raise their eyebrows. Humble people are surprised if he behaves in a human way. I once had a letter from a Muganda expressing great joy because I had sat on a sofa with him, a private person, at a tea party when I was on tour. The ignorant are surprised if he works hard; some art students from Makerere College who came to lunch with us in Entebbe were told that I was late for lunch because I was working; afterwards one of them remarked that he did not know Governors ever worked. A Governor must within reason be available to all types of people and he must be ready to grace many occasions both great and small. It is in fact his task to represent to the public the human side of the Government machine.

Not only that; he is the Chief Executive until at a very advanced stage of constitutional development he hands over this responsibility to an elected Prime Minister. Until then the Governor chooses his Ministers and takes the initiative in the formation of policy. Before the war the Governor's influence inside the machine was even more powerful than it has been since. Admittedly he had to pay close attention to local opinion as expressed in the Legislature and elsewhere; he would have neglected it at his peril, particularly in Kenya and the Gold Coast. But, inside the machine, the Chief Secretary and the Secretariat had no real existence independent of the Governor. Admittedly the Chief Secretary as a member of Executive Council could have a dissenting view recorded if he disagreed entirely with the Governor; in practice this rarely if ever happened. Even in a large Territory the scope of the work was not too great for the Governor to concern himself with all fields of activity, although it frequently happened that successive Governors took an interest in different things—native administration, economic development, or education, thus shifting the emphasis of Government policy. The Chief Secretary and the Secretariat could and often did influence the Governor greatly: they could restrain him or stimulate him, or of course just follow him. Some Governors came to a Territory with little knowledge of its local affairs; one was once described to me by one of his advisers as being so knowledgeable on all subjects that he always knew more than they did on whatever came up. I have known Governors who operated as the head of a team, influencing their officers, securing agreement, and then letting their subordinates do the running. I have known others who dominated the scene and largely determined policy themselves.

THE GOVERNOR AND THE COLONIAL OFFICE

In his dealings with the Secretary of State and the Colonial Office at the time when I first joined the Service in the early 1930's, the Governor was in a very strong position. It is true that he was entirely responsible to the Secretary of State who appointed him; but he alone knew the changing local situation and the local personalities. Very largely the initiative was in his hands. The relationship between the Secretary of State and Colonial Governors may be of some interest, and I am perhaps in a good position to talk about it, having served both in the

Colonial Office and as a Governor. I therefore propose to deal with this question at some length.

The Colonial Office in the 1930's

I will begin by explaining what the Colonial Office was like 25 years ago. It was of course a much smaller organization than it is today. It consisted mainly of geographical departments, i.e., those dealing with a particular area, such as East Africa or the West Indies. Apart from the sections dealing with the Colonial Service, it had few functional departments; the Economic Section of the Colonial Office was only just starting up in the 1930's and had only two officers at that time.

The Colonial Office is part of the Home Civil Service, not the Colonial Service. Its officers, who are recruited by a very stiff competitive examination, were always extremely knowledgeable on paper about the areas they dealt with. But at that time they might never have set foot in the Territory in question or even in any colonial Territory. One or two of the older ones prided themselves on not having done so, although in the 1930's an arrangement was introduced under which every new administrative officer in the Colonial Office had to spend two of his first five years in a Territory. Contacts with the Territories were a good deal less close than they are now, and much of the correspondence with Governments was conducted by the decorous but somewhat leisurely method of exchanging dispatches. Governors had to get formal approval from the Colonial Office for quite a number of relatively unimportant things, such as details of expenditure. On some of the larger issues of policy, though they had to consult the Colonial Office, they were in fact left relatively free. There was no one in the Colonial Office who was expert on the subject of native administration, and

I remember being surprised early in my service at being asked to write a note describing our policy on this.

Generally speaking, except on technical questions and on economic matters, in which, as I have said, the Colonial Office was just beginning to take a more active hand, the Office did not take the initiative in laying down or propounding policy. It awaited dispatches from Governors proposing policy in this or that field and then advised the Secretary of State on the answer to be sent. This was done by a series of minutes, often lengthy, as the file in question ascended the hierarchy. Broadly speaking the tendency was to accept the advice of the man on the spot unless there was some positive reason to the contrary. I do not want to give the impression that the Colonial Office was not a powerful influence on policy and action; obviously it was. The Office used this influence, if necessary, to prevent a Governor from going off the rails on a matter of policy; but very largely the Governor supplied the motive power. This was not of course the result of inertia or indifference in the Colonial Office; leaving the initiative to the man on the spot was part of the traditional British attitude towards overseas administration.

The British Press and Parliamentary Opinion

The freedom the Colonial Office left to Governors was partly due to the relative lack of interest in Africa then taken by the British press and to the fact that interest in Parliament, although considerable, was much less widespread than it became later. Parliament had admittedly always taken an interest in major issues of African policy. The report of the Joint Select Committee of Parliament in 1931 on Closer Union in East Africa is an example of this; other examples are the long argument over land in Kenya and the cocoa holdup on the Gold Coast in the late 1930's. Some Members of Parliament on both sides of the House took a close interest in African problems; a smaller number visited Africa occasionally. But the attendance at colonial debates was poor and, by modern standards, the number of parliamentary questions was small.

After the Second World War the position changed, and public interest in Africa increased enormously. The press, both daily and weekly, is full of articles on African subjects. Colonial affairs are one of the most fruitful subjects for parliamentary questions. There is no Colonial Committee of the House of Commons, because standing committees of this type are not part of our parliamentary system. The setting up of such a Committee has sometimes been suggested, partly with a view to producing a bipartisan colonial policy, but the idea has always been resisted by the Government in office and the Colonial Office, partly no doubt because it is felt that the existence of such a Committee would complicate the already delicate relationship with local Legislatures and political parties. Members of Parliament have many chances of getting to know colonial leaders and problems. Visits by Members to African Territories are frequent and political leaders from the Territories see Members when they come to London. Both the Conservative and the Labour Party have research organizations dealing with colonial affairs. Both publish pamphlets on the subject.

The Post-War Colonial Office

To match this greatly increased interest the Colonial Office itself emerged from the war with a much larger staff and more elaborate organization. This was partly because the task of conducting the external relations of the dependent Territories had become a much more extensive one in the post-war world. In the political field the United Nations, and in particular the Trusteeship system and Chapter XI of the Charter dealing with non-self-governing Territories, created a new field of activity for the Office to handle. In the economic and social fields the more closely organized conditions of the post-war world, and in particular the Specialized Agencies of the United Nations, the G.A.T.T., the O.E.E.C. and the whole subject of civil aviation, added further responsibilities.

The new positive policy of economic and social development greatly increased the work of the Office, which handles British Government grants under the Colonial Development and Welfare Acts, the raising of loans on the London market by Colonial Governments, and the expansion of research services. An enormous recruiting effort had to be made to support the new policy. Since 1945 over 2,000 administrators, 2,500 teachers, 1,500 doctors, 2,000 engineers, and 3,000 other officers of graduate quality have been recruited by the Colonial Office for service in the Territories in Africa and elsewhere. Centralized topographic and geological surveys were set up to operate in the Territories. The specialized advisory services of the Colonial Office in technical fields and the advisory committees of distinguished experts in these fields—services which had been important before the war—became even more so after the war and were greatly expanded. Distinguished scientists in all disciplines have given their services on these specialized committees and their advice on the establishment and staffing of research institutions in the Territories. The heads of all the universities and many of the technical colleges in Britain made themselves available—and have indeed devoted a great deal of their time—to help the new colleges in Africa and elsewhere to establish themselves. The Colonial Development Corporation was set up to promote industrial, mineral, agricultural, and commercial projects in the Territories. Although some of these new organizations deal direct with the Governments abroad, the policy under which they operate is laid down by the Secretary of State through the Colonial Office.

In fact, since the war the Office has been undertaking a whole series of new functions which, because they involve either the external relations of Colonial Territories, or the expenditure of United Kingdom money in the Territories, or the application of expert advice from the United Kingdom to the affairs of the Territories, have inevitably involved the Office in a much greater degree of initiative in its dealings with Governments over a wide field of activity. The rapid constitutional development which has taken place during the period has inevitably had the same effect; because clearly in major constitutional reform the United Kingdom Government, through its responsibility to the British Parliament, must play the leading part. The Secretary of State for the Colonies has come to have a very special personal role to play—and to some extent a new one—in constitutional development. As the political leaders in Africa and elsewhere have gained both power and influence, constitutional reform has increasingly been settled in discussion with them. Such discussion has to a very large extent been conducted by the Secretary of State personally with the help of the Governor concerned; without the presence of the Secretary of State it would have lost much of its point. Examples of this are the Nigerian Conferences of 1953 and 1954 under Mr. Lyttelton's chairmanship and that of 1957 under Mr. Lennox-Boyd's; and the discussions with leaders of all races leading to constitutional reform in Kenya by Mr. Griffiths in 1951, by Mr. Lyttelton in 1954, and by Mr. Lennox-Boyd in 1957.

During this period steps were taken to remove some of the formal controls by the Colonial Office over African Governments; for example local control by Public Accounts Committees was substituted for supervision by the Colonial Office of the expenditure, accounts, etc. of the Governments. At the same time in a field which had been largely left to local initiative, that of native administration, the Colonial Office after the war began to take a more active hand in policy-making. Lord Hailey's study of this subject had shown the need to bring the policy of indirect rule up to date. The Colonial Office during the 1940's gave a great deal of attention to the whole matter, as it has done since. An African Studies Branch was established at the Colonial Office to help keep policy under review and to circulate information to Governments; the *Journal of African Administration* was founded to keep the Service informed of new developments and problems; panels of specialists were set up to advise the Office on problems affecting local government and native courts.

Proposals for new policy on local government were set out, as I have already said, in a circular dispatch from the Secretary of State in 1947. The idea was that in modern conditions policy-making in this vital matter could no longer be left purely to local initiative in any given Territory. A broad general policy was to be laid down, based on full discussion between the Colonial Office and the Governments in Africa; experienced officers from the field who knew the whole subject from the practical point of view were to take part in these discussions. It was within this framework of policy that individual field officers were to be given flexibility of action, as I have already explained; great importance was attached by the Colonial Office to flexibility of action in the field. To discuss the whole policy of local government, the first Cambridge Conference was held in the summer of 1947. This was attended by most of the leading officials dealing with native administration in the Territories and by many other officers. A whole series of recommendations was agreed upon, and these general principles were again discussed and studied at a conference with Governors of African Territories held in London by Mr. Creech-Jones in 1948. The Colonial Office also took the initiative in proposing policy in the sphere of community development (sometimes called mass or fundamental education), and later on land tenure and the establishment of individual land titles for Africans, on which some very good work has been done in conferences held by the Colonial Office at Cambridge and in Tanganyika.

The Secretary of State and the Governor Since the War

What effect have all these things had on the part played by Governors in the formation of policy? The speed of communications, the frequent journeys to Africa by the Secretary of State and his senior officials and to London by Governors and senior officers of Governments, the many conferences have brought London and the African capitals much closer together. The greatly increased interest in Africa taken by Parliament and the British press, the growing international interest, the positive policy of economic and social development, the important constitutional reforms made during the period—all these things have combined to make it inevitable that the Colonial Office should take more initiative in policy-making.

At the same time the increase in political activity in the Territories and the growth of political parties, the increasingly representative character of Legislatures and the spread of direct elections, and most important of all the introduction of responsible government in West Africa and of membership and later ministerial systems in East Africa—all these things have combined to create a local political personality in the Territories and to insure that the political balance did not shift away from them and that the weight of the Governor's own contribution to the forming of policy was not lessened. Inside Governments in Africa the Governor's personal part in the details of policy-making has often tended to diminish as Members or Ministers took responsibility for this or that sphere of activity. But the

Governor's task as a coordinator and political conciliator increased correspondingly, and dealings between the Colonial Office and Governments on major issues tended less and less to be conducted through formal written exchanges and more and more through personal discussions and correspondence between the Governor on the one hand and the Secretary of State and Colonial Office on the other.

In fact I think it is fair to say that a balance has been maintained between local initiative on the part of the Governor and central direction from London. Certainly Governors have continued to take the initiative in putting forward policy proposals, and the sphere of operation over which Governments have had virtually complete freedom of action has not diminished, indeed rather the reverse. With the continually growing scope of activity by Governments in Africa and with the political developments taking place during the period, the fields in which London does not actively concern itself have probably been steadily increasing all the time. Thus, although Africa came closer to London, as it did to the rest of the world, and although consultation became both more frequent and more rapid, there was no reversal during this period of the classical British policy of devolution. Governments continued to develop as separate if controlled units, so that when responsibility was handed over, as in West Africa, to locally elected Ministers, the transition was on the whole a remarkably smooth one.

FOUR

Africa and the West: Needs of the Future

IN EARLIER talks I have dealt mainly with political and administrative problems of the past and present. I would now like to look at the future in terms of the help from the outside world which the African countries need for their economic and social development and will continue to need as far ahead as we can foresee both before they get self-government and afterwards. I shall end by discussing the attitude which the Western world should take to the problems of material aid to these countries of tropical Africa.

The objective in the economic and social fields is not essentially different for the West and East African Territories, in spite of their being at different stages of political advance. It is simply this, that when they get self-government they should be able to stand on their feet as viable states in the modern world. For this purpose political progress must be accompanied by economic development so as to raise national income and the standard of living, and by educational and social advance in order to produce leaders who can run the public life of the country, its commerce, and its professions. British policy has therefore been three-pronged. Political progress, economic development, and educational and social advance are interdependent. None can succeed without the other two.

AN AFRICAN ECONOMY

I am going to illustrate the needs of these countries by describing very briefly the economy of the one I know best, Uganda. It is not typical in all respects, because it has a better rainfall and a more fertile soil than some African countries, but it will serve to bring out the main points.

The great majority of the people of Uganda are peasant farmers living not in towns or villages, but in houses or huts scattered over the countryside. They grow not only food, but also cotton and coffee for export and groundnuts and tobacco for local sale. There are only very small areas where no cash crops are grown. In many parts of the country cattle are kept as well, but large areas are barred to cattle by the tsetse fly, although the Government has reclaimed parts of these from the fly in recent years and protected others from its onset by control measures. Most cattle owners still send their stock to market only to a limited extent; but with the growing internal trade in meat the sales are steadily increasing. Only a small part of the country is overpopulated and even there the overcrowding is less acute than in parts of Kenya and Eastern Nigeria. In most parts of Uganda the soil is not as light as in many parts of Africa and less subject to erosion; in many areas soil conservation measures have been taken to protect the land.

Farm labor is mostly provided by the family, largely by the women. Plows, introduced by the British administration, are only used in some places; tractors are popular, but have only been introduced recently and in many areas are probably not economic. The Government agricultural and veterinary field services have done a remarkable job in helping the people to improve their methods, but crop yields remain low. The people live mostly on small farms of not more than ten acres, holding their land by right of occupation under native custom. Except in Buganda the ownership of the land is communal, although in overcrowded areas individual tenure is increasingly recognized by custom. In Buganda a form of freehold tenure was established under the 1900 Agreement and there are now some 50,000 landowners, some of them large, many of them small; tenants have legal security of tenure, a good arrangement socially but not conducive to improvement of the land. Only about half of 1% of the land in Uganda is alienated to Europeans or Indians, and plantation agriculture is on a small scale only. All the cotton and the great majority of the coffee is peasant-produced. Tea and sugar are plantation crops.

Cotton and coffee account for nearly 90 per cent of the country's exports, so that the economy is vulnerable to changes in world prices. Mining, mostly for tin and wolfram, was until recently done on a small scale; but a new copper mine has now been opened and plans are being made to develop an important phosphate and niobium deposit. The main industry is processing—cotton ginning and coffee curing. Like the smaller industries of brewing and the manufacture of building and household materials, these are for the most part in the hands of Indians, with some European concerns taking part; but with direct assistance from Government Africans have now been brought into them. Recently cement and textile factories have been established, both operated by the publicly financed Uganda Development Corporation. There are few African entrepreneurs and managers, although the number is increasing.

The cotton and the great majority of the coffee crops are bought locally and sold overseas by Marketing Boards established by the Government under statute. The African co-operative movement has become an important factor in primary marketing. But this, as well as the import, export, and whole-sale trades, is largely in the hands of Indians and Europeans. Retail trade is also mainly in the hands of Indians; but the African share in this is increasing, and over 15,000 African retail traders now carry on almost half the country's retail trade. Combined with the rapid spread of the cooperative movement, the growing number of substantial African farmers, and the advance of Africans in the professions, this is steadily building up an African middle class. Many fine houses have been built in the richer areas of the countryside; I know one area in Buganda where there are more cars than taxpayers. The money income of Africans throughout the country more than doubled between 1950 and 1956, and in that year this repre-sented 65 per cent of the total money income of the country or three-quarters of the geographical income if African sub-sistence agriculture is included. The geographical income in real terms has been increasing at the rate of about 5 per cent per year.

Towns are growing, but are still small, and Uganda has so far largely escaped the problems of the big modern or in-dustrial centers so familiar in other parts of Africa. Only a little over 5 per cent of the population is in paid employment. Peas-ant farmers with an income from cash crops normally do not work for wages and most of the unskilled labor comes from areas without cash crops in the extreme northwest or south-west of the country or from Ruanda Urundi. Many Baganda farmers employ Banyaruanda migrant labor on their farms. Many of the skilled artisans are Asians; increasing numbers of African artisans are now coming out of the technical schools, but there is still an acute shortage of them. A great drive is going for-ward to increase and improve primary, secondary, and university education, both academic and technical, but there are still far too few candidates with secondary school or higher qualifications. Any young man or woman with a secondary or even a junior secondary education can be sure of a choice of work.

Uganda has a good trunk road system, better than most tropical African countries; but much new road construction is needed. There is a good coverage of subsidiary roads in the central areas, less good in the rest of the country. Uganda has no local fuel resources and the Nile has therefore been dammed to produce electric power. Although the country is relatively well-watered, there are many areas with inadequate water supplies for men and cattle; a large program of dam and well construction is going forward. Research services have been built up, either in Uganda itself or on an interterritorial East African basis; but there is very much still to be learned about the methods of dealing with the physical problems of the country.

DEFICIENCIES IN THE AFRICAN ECONOMY

This brief picture is of a country with a mainly peasant economy—having the strengths and weaknesses which such an economy usually shows. It is of a country engaged in building up its basic utilities, developing new industries, improving and extending its education, and helping Africans to expand from production into other economic activities. Some gaps are apparent in the picture; in this Uganda is essentially no different from other tropical African countries, or indeed from undeveloped countries in other parts of the world. These gaps point the way to the action which the outside world can take to help these countries; I would like therefore to give a list of them.

1. Low productivity of peasant agriculture.
2. Lack in most areas of a system of individual land tenure.
3. Insufficient basic utilities owing to insufficient capital for investment.
4. Lack of balance in the economy of the country.
5. Instability in the prices of the country's main products.
6. Limited African part in commerce and industry; lack of entrepreneurs and managers among Africans.
7. Need for more scientific knowledge of the problems and potentialities of the country.
8. Insufficient numbers of highly educated men and women and of skilled artisans.

I propose now to say a few words about each of these gaps, not specially in relation to Uganda, but dealing with these countries generally.

Low Productivity of Peasant Agriculture

Because peasant agriculture often produces low crop yields, the question is sometimes asked whether it would not be better to organize farming on the basis of plantations managed for the present by experts from overseas. The answer is that, however efficient plantation agriculture may be, however valuable in certain areas, peasant agriculture must in the foreseeable future be the mainstay of tropical Africa. In overcrowded areas there is no room for plantations; in many other areas African opposition to land alienation would prevent their development. Peasant farming has the advantage of spreading the wealth from cash crops widely among the people, and this makes for both economic and political stability.

There is much that governments can do to help peasant

farmers increase their efficiency, so as to secure, quite apart from any new land which may be brought under cultivation, that more is produced per acre from the area already farmed. A comparatively small increase in the average yield per acre from cotton in Uganda—an increase which is certainly possible —would produce more wealth than much more grandiose projects. The task is essentially one for agricultural and veterinary field or extension services, for farm institutes and agricultural teaching in schools. The need is to persuade the farmers to cultivate in the right way, to take the correct measures against disease, to organize their farming operations properly. The job is to apply modern techniques and scientific knowledge to the practical operations of farming. It is a task which requires leadership as well as education, one in which the leaders of the people, both traditional and elected, can play an effective part in cooperation with Government officers. To carry out this task Government must have at its disposal highly trained scientists to work in research organizations, experimental stations, and the field. Since at present most of these officers must be recruited from overseas, the training of local officers to fill these positions is of the first importance. At the same time large numbers of local field staff must be trained in the Territories, from men having farm institute diplomas down to the lower staff working in the villages.

Lack of a System of Individual Land Tenure

An individual title to land recognized under statutory law and not simply by native custom can be a great incentive to better farming and the improvement of the land. Lack of such a title prevents a farmer from getting credit on the security of his land, and this has interfered with the various schemes which

Governments have introduced to make credit available to Africans. These things are now generally recognized, and in Kenya much progress has been made among the Kikuyu since the Mau Mau emergency in securing the agreement of the people to individual tenure.

No Government can hope to succeed in introducing changes affecting land unless they are understood and accepted by the African people. The whole subject must be handled with the utmost caution, as it has been up to now. Land is the basis of life in Africa as elsewhere and Africans are intensely suspicious on all matters affecting land. Unfortunately there has been some opposition to land reform in some parts of Kenya. Proposals for individual tenure which we put forward in Uganda also met with opposition in some places, although they were most carefully explained by the Minister of Land Tenure, himself an African, and by other people. In one place it was said, "The Government is going to divide up our land and give it out to us in little parcels; they will take the rest away for their own purposes, perhaps for European settlement." Of course there was no truth in this fear of our taking the land away, as anyone who had studied the proposals could see; but distortions such as this illustrate the immense difficulty a colonial administration has in securing changes in land tenure.

Certain other things are essential to success in land reform. The proper African Authorities must be associated with the grant of individual title. Africans who get such a title must be prevented from alienating their land to people of other races without proper permission. Governments have an inescapable duty to protect African land rights, both present and future, and it would be no answer to criticism to say that a given landowner had agreed to lease his land. Individual tenure, at this stage at any rate should only be considered for areas specially suited to it; there may be a number of areas which are not. The evils of agricultural debt which have been known in many parts of Asia must be kept away from Africa; if land is pledged as security, it must be for loans from Government-owned credit banks, or at any rate banks operating under a properly regulated system providing for public supervision. Given all these things, it is not to be expected, even so, that changes in land tenure can be introduced except after a long process of public enlightenment and discussion. Nevertheless individual tenure is necessary for economic progress, at any rate in many areas; here again Governments and the leaders of the people are faced with a task of persuasion and education.

Insufficient Basic Utilities

The basic economic services essential to development are communications-roads, railroads and ports; electric power; water supplies; irrigation and drainage schemes; and urban services, including African housing schemes. Under African conditions these are services to be developed by Governments, since none of these countries has local sources of private capital large enough to tackle them, and capital from overseas investing in underdeveloped countries looks to a quicker and higher return than public utilities can provide. Investment by Governments in these projects is indeed unlikely to produce a direct return quickly in the shape of increased revenue, except in very special cases, as for example when a railroad is built to carry heavy mineral traffic from a new mine. But in the long run all these basic utilities, if properly planned, will raise national income and government revenue by stimulating development. Feeder roads and improved water supplies, as well as irrigation and drainage schemes, open up new land for economic crops; trunk roads and improved urban services stimulate internal and external trade; electric power is needed for industrial and mining development; railroads and ports must be modernized and provided with the necessary carrying capacity to support economic development generally.

All the Governments of British Africa have carried through large projects for the improvement of basic services since 1948, partly financed from local revenue and surplus funds, partly from loans raised overseas, and partly from grants by the British Government under the Colonial Development and Welfare Acts. Since 1950, to take one example, the Uganda Government has invested over $60 million in hydro-electric power, with more expansion planned; $15 million has been put into railroad construction, over and above the very large general program of railroad and port improvement carried out by the East African Railways. The Uganda Government has also been investing about $3 million a year in road construction, about $1 million a year in improving water supplies and comparable sums in urban services including African housing.

These investments, large though they are by tropical African standards, could be increased if more capital were available. When development has gone much further, local investment must produce the major part of the capital needed, and a start has already been made in tapping local sources. But Africans will only gradually acquire the practice of investing, whether in companies or in public loans. Many countries more developed than those in Africa continue to rely on a large measure of outside investment. If the tropical African Territories are to be brought in a reasonable time to the stage when they can sustain their own development, they will need, and need quickly, very large amounts of capital from outside.

Lack of Balance in the Economy

Like Uganda, most of the countries of tropical Africa depend on one or two main export crops, sometimes with a limited degree of mineral development; the Belgian Congo is a striking exception to this. With greater or lesser success these countries have been trying to diversify their economies by encouraging new mining and secondary industries. This is mainly a task for private enterprise, and to a very large extent at the present stage private enterprise from overseas which alone has the know-how. Governments have an essential contribution to make in providing the basic utilities I have already described. In the case of mining these include geological survey, and for this purpose the United Kingdom Government has organized a centrally controlled service which employs geologists in all the Territories.

The greater part of the very large outside investment in Africa since the war has gone into the countries with large or relatively large European populations and with mines and industries already established, in particular the Union of South Africa, the Federation of Rhodesia and Nyasaland, and the Belgian Congo. Among British tropical African Territories Kenya attracts outside investment more easily than Tanganyika, Uganda, or the West African Territories. This is not, I believe, because of any political preference on the part of outside investors. They are of course interested in the political stability of the countries in which they invest, but would not necessarily take the view that independent countries controlled by Africans were in general likely to be less stable in the long run than others. The handicap most tropical African countries suffer from is the limited numbers of local managers and entrepreneurs, the small numbers of trained artisans, and the fact that there are few local financial institutions. Like calls to like, and potential investors tend to find countries with more Europeans established in them closer to their own experience. Therefore in nearly all the tropical African countries the problem of industrial and mining development is not simply one of investing enough capital and providing enough skilled personnel from outside; it is a question of training local technicians, managers, and skilled workers, and at the same time creating conditions which will attract private investors into these countries.

One way of doing this is by Governments themselves participating in mining or industrial development; indeed sometimes outside companies make this a condition of investing in a new project. The Kilembe copper mine in Uganda was partly financed by an issue on the Toronto Stock Exchange, I believe the largest issue so far made in Canada for a mining venture outside that country. Commercial men connected with the project said that this successful issue was only possible because the Government was in the project. Participation by the Governments in mining or industrial ventures should normally be made through an organization operated on commercial lines; it was for this purpose that the Uganda Government set up the Uganda Development Corporation. Such a Corporation also helps to give confidence to African public opinion, for Africans feel that it is holding their share of development projects through the use of public funds.

In the conditions of most of these countries the development of secondary industries is bound to be difficult. The lack of skilled labor and shortage of local technical staff, the limited scale of local utilities, and the lack of general development may make it difficult for a new industry to compete with the products of highly industrialized countries, even allowing for the transport differential. To meet this Governments may have to give special inducements to a new industry, such as exemption from income tax in the initial stages or the right to import essential supplies free of customs duty. A measure of protection or even some degree of subsidy may also be justified for a limited period. But the building up of industry must not be treated as an end in itself. It is better to go without an industry which is not economic in the long run than to put an economic millstone round the neck of a country indefinitely. For this reason industrial development is likely to progress slowly and, unless large mining deposits are proved which can be worked economically, these countries are likely to go on depending principally on a comparatively small number of agricultural products.

Instability of Prices

This makes it all the more important that prices should be stable. Since the war Statutory Boards set up by Governments have been much used for marketing some of the principal crops. Cocoa has been marketed in this way in Ghana; cocoa, palm products, and groundnuts in Nigeria; and, as I have said, cotton and coffee in Uganda. The growers have been guaranteed prices fixed annually by the Governments, and short term fluctuations have to a considerable extent been avoided. During the war and after it, and in some cases even now, these prices have been fixed well below the equivalent of the world price, and the Boards have built up large price stabilization funds; substantial export taxes have also been levied by Governments on these crops when they are sold through Marketing Boards.

The system has been criticized by some laissez faire economists. I am not, of course, concerned here about the way in which it has been worked in any particular country, nor am I qualified to argue with economists. But, as one who has dealt with the affairs of all these countries and governed one of them, I am in no doubt that the principle of Marketing Boards and guaranteed prices has been fully justified. Stability in prices tends to encourage production, and the fixing of guaranteed prices each year before the planting season is useful where crops are planted annually, as in the case of cotton. Experience before the war both in West Africa and Uganda shows the unsettling effect of fluctuating world prices when the producer is not insulated from them. The fixing of prices to producers at levels below the world price was a measure against inflation; the prices actually paid were in any case far above the pre-war level, even allowing for changes in the value of money. The surplus funds accumulated by the Boards over and above the amounts needed for price stabilization have been used for economic and social development for the benefit of the people as a whole—certainly a far better use for these very large sums of money than if they had been distributed in small amounts each year to individual growers. Indeed the social and economic progress of Ghana, Nigeria, and Uganda has depended to a very large extent on this source of finance.

Stabilization funds can insulate growers from short term price fluctuations. But neither they nor any other measures taken by African Governments can protect either the growers or the countries from the effects of major falls in prices of raw materials. Such major changes are entirely outside their control and could have a disastrous effect on the development of the African countries. Admittedly they profited from the high prices ruling during the war and immediately after it; but the recent falls in the prices of many of their staple exports have already sharply reduced the amount of money available for development and have in fact made it necessary for development programs to be slowed down. Here is a possible field for international action to help the whole process of development in Africa.

Limited African Part in Commerce and Industry: Lack of Entrepreneurs and Managers among Africans

In the East African Territories Africans have thus far played a comparatively small part in retail trade and a still smaller part in wholesale trade and industry. With the bulk of the population taking only a small part in commercial activity, not only is the economic progress of a country bound to be retarded, but social and political frictions occur. The Governments have therefore felt it necessary to take positive steps to help Africans in these fields. In Uganda, believing this to be a matter of urgency, we put in hand a positive program for the advancement of Africans in trade, through instruction to individuals in trading methods, loans to traders on economic terms to help them develop their business, the formation of associations of traders for mutual advantage, and the provision of wholesale and transport services to provide the needs of African traders. To encourage wholesalers to operate in outlying areas the Government put up wholesale showrooms, and considerable sums were invested by Government to build shops in the main towns for rent to Africans on economic terms. Formal education—commercial, technical, and general—is, of course, part of the process, but success in business can come only with actual experience.

Any positive program of this kind is necessarily slow and beset with pitfalls, but much can be achieved by arranging for traders who get loans from Government credit agencies to be given expert advice and guidance, by training promising African staff inside business firms, and by partnership or management arrangements between European or Asian firms and African companies with the object of helping the African partners with capital and know-how and training them and their employees in management. Another important field, which has not yet been sufficiently explored, is the encouragement of small industries producing for the local market, with the help of loans from public or even private sources to individual Africans, companies, or groups. Such schemes have two advantages: they help to spread development widely over the country; and they stimulate internal trade and the local market—which should always be one of the aims of economic policy.

An effective means of bringing Africans into new economic activity has been the cooperative movement, in which societies mostly composed of farmers work under the guidance of trained Government officials operating on recognized cooperative principles. In all the Territories, both in West and East Africa, the cooperative movement has grown and flourished. In Uganda the movement started some ten years ago, and there are now over 1,400 societies with twelve Cooperative Unions and an annual turnover estimated at over $14 million. Cooperative Unions now operate eleven cotton ginneries in Uganda, which they have acquired with substantial assistance from public funds by way of long term loans. Cooperative Unions and African companies have also acquired coffee-curing plants under the same arrangements. The object of all these schemes, both in Uganda and elsewhere, is to encourage the growth of an African middle class playing an increasing part in economic activity and to help Africans gain knowledge of commerce and industry through training and actual experience. Measures for the advancement of Africans in trade and the cooperative movement are both important parts of the education program in its widest sense.

Need for More Scientific Knowledge

It is clearly most important that, in the period of growth towards self-government, scientific research services should be firmly established and allowed to prove their value to the people of the Territories and their leaders. Great emphasis has been laid on this in British policy, as in Belgian and French. Large grants have been and are still being made by the British Government for this purpose, and the best scientific brains in Britain have helped with their advice and often by working or organizing work in the field. In East Africa, to take one region only, there are research institutes for agriculture, forestry, veterinary science, fisheries, tripanosomiasis and the control of the tsetse fly, virus diseases, nutrition, social and economic research, and industrial and technological research. In the vital agricultural field better strains of crops and better measures against disease are constantly being developed. The effect of climate and rainfall on soil and the correct rotation of crops and fallow is continuously being studied. Research is going forward into the problems of rehabilitating desiccated or eroded areas, a thing of first importance if these countries are to continue to be able to produce enough food for their rising populations. Scientific investigations to prepare new economic projects are also constantly being put in hand. One to study the prospects of drainage and irrigation in the great Rufiji River Basin in Tanganyika is being conducted by the United Nations Food and Agricultural Organization. Remarkable results have been achieved from research in Africa, which have already contributed greatly to the development of these Territories. But very large areas of knowledge still remain to be conquered.

The Training of Leaders

Neither the building up of the institutions of modern countries, nor the increasing of national wealth, nor even the growth of knowledge will achieve effective results without the development of the human potential in Africa. The most important part of building a nation is the production of leaders, which involves bringing forward young African men and women with an education good enough to enable them to play leading parts in public life, the civil service, local government, the professions, business, and industry, as leaders of cooperative movements and trade unions, as community leaders, and as women's leaders. Without an educated and efficient local leadership in public life, administration, and economic affairs, the development of these countries is bound to be retarded, because there is a limit to what can be achieved by an outside body of administrators and managers whether in dependent or independent countries. And, after independence, outside financial and technical help will only be effective to the extent that there is an efficient local administrative machine.

Thus education in the widest sense is vital. In the British Territories of West and East Africa three University Colleges have been established and four Higher Colleges giving general and technical education. There has been a great expansion of secondary and primary schools which provide the intake for the universities, of technical schools to train artisans and technicians, of teacher training colleges to provide the machine tools for all educational advance, and of adult education and community development work. Campaigns to promote health education have been mounted. A special effort has been made by all Governments to increase the number of Africans in the higher levels of the civil service, which still rely largely on officers from overseas. Schemes to help local candidates to obtain the necessary qualifications either in Africa or overseas are operating in every Territory.

These are beginning to produce substantial results in East Africa and have already done so in West Africa. There are now over 5,000 students of all sorts from East and West Africa in Britain and many in the United States. The great amount which remains to be done is shown by the fact that in Uganda, as advanced in education as any Territory on the eastern side of Africa, the annual turnout of the top class of the secondary schools will only be about 800 by 1960 and that of the University College of Makerere under a hundred students from Uganda; this in spite of increases of nearly 200% in the number of students in secondary schools and at Makerere. It is vital to the future of these countries that this great educational effort be sustained.

Education can, of course, do no more than provide the material for leaders. Leaders and efficient managers and administrators will emerge only through the exercise of responsibility and the gaining of practical experience; hence the great importance of giving larger and larger numbers of Africans practical experience in public affairs both centrally and in local government. Training the people to run their own countries has, I believe, been the main distinguishing characteristic of British administration in Africa.

THE NEEDS OF THE FUTURE

The countries of tropical Africa have adopted the methods of progress of the Western world—a cash economy, western economic and educational systems, and western political institutions. In the last two generations they have been transformed, and in the last fifteen years in particular their progress has been very rapid. But it would be foolish and irresponsible not to recognize what a vast amount remains to be done in social and economic development. Because the advanced countries of the world are so much richer, the gap between their national wealth and that of underdeveloped countries is not narrowing but tending to widen, even though the rate of economic growth of the latter relative to the scale of their own economies may be greater than that of developed countries. As Mr. Adlai Stevenson has written:

> Like Alice and the Red Queen, the new nations of Asia and Africa have to run faster and faster just to stay where they are. Yet they find it difficult to maintain even the pace already set; they certainly cannot keep up with their advancing needs unless they receive more economic assistance from highly-developed nations. To become and remain truly independent these "have-not" nations must grow economically strong, a fact well realized by their leaders who are combing the world for credits and capital.

The changes and improvements which are needed cannot be made in a day; they will take years to accomplish. In dependent Territories, which we want to leave as strong as possible when they get their independence, the tasks of economic and social development have a special urgency, because we no longer have indefinite time in front of us. But countries which have achieved their independence also need outside assistance. The social and economic problems which face them are not solved by independence, nor can the grant of independence be delayed until they have been solved.

Independence may indeed release new local energies and pride to tackle the tasks of development, but it may at the same time turn off some earlier taps of outside capital and technical assistance. For example British dependent Territories when they become independent no longer qualify for Colonial Development and Welfare grants or new investment by the Colonial Development Corporation, although they do receive technical assistance from Britain and come within the field of the Commonwealth Development Finance Company. They can no longer raise loans in the London or other markets or from the International Bank under the actual or implied guarantee of the British Government. Although they can of course continue to employ British officials—the Ghana Government has recently taken special steps to encourage these to remain—they no longer make use of the recruitment machinery of the British Government and in the nature of things they are bound to lose many of their British officers. New methods of helping them suitable to their new status and of course acceptable to them may therefore have to be worked out. The encouraging thing is that they themselves recognize their continuing need for outside aid and are ready and anxious to receive it.

Certain principles are important in the granting of outside aid. It should not be treated as a continuing subsidy of the recurrent costs of government services in an underdeveloped country. It should be designed as an injection from outside at key points of the economy to stimulate the development of national wealth and government revenue, initially so that the country can support the expansion of public services and developments of all sorts and can attract private capital from outside, and later so as to help increase its economic strength to the point when it "takes off" economically and can sustain its further economic growth largely from its own savings and resources. Countries granting aid have the right to expect that receiving countries will themselves contribute adequately to their own development and that they will take measures to ensure that aid is efficiently used and that it benefits the country and the public generally and not simply one privileged class.

Subject to these principles aid should, in my view, be concentrated on the following objects which clearly emerge from the analysis I have given earlier:

1 *Loans for basic utilities.* The building up of the basic services of a country is clearly one of the most suitable objects for outside assistance and this is likely to take the form of loans from the International Bank and from Governments and other public sources. Means should be found of making some of these loans at medium or low rates of interest and with easy repayment terms to finance projects, particularly in the field of communications, which are only likely to produce a full return after a period of years.

2 *Loans for economic projects.* Government or public loans may also legitimately be used to supplement or support private investment, whether from local or overseas sources, in industrial, mining, commercial, and agricultural projects. Investment from local sources can be helped by credit schemes designed particularly for small industries or other projects of a kind likely to be attractive to Africans. Private investment from overseas would be helped by the setting up of liaison machinery to keep governments and other interested people in the African Territories informed of potential overseas investors and of the conditions they are likely to require for investing their capital, and to keep the potential investors informed of opportunities and conditions in the African countries. This liaison could be provided by the Development Corporations operating in some of the Territories through their overseas contacts, but it also seems necessary that the African countries should employ suitable liaison staff in the main centers abroad from which investment may be expected.

3 *Stabilizing world prices of raw materials.* Until development is much further advanced, the economies of most of the African Territories and their prospects of development are highly vulnerable, as I have said, to major falls in the world prices of their main exports. I do not propose to discuss here

how such price fluctations could be minimized; but, if international action could successfully achieve this, it would be doing far more for the advancement of the people of Africa than many of the more sterile discussions which now take place in some international bodies.

4 *The promotion of research.* Help from outside is likely to be specially needed for developing research services, because the African countries themselves can only be expected to produce a small number of highly trained scientists at the present stage, given the competition which exists in them for the services of their best brains. Fundamental research, which is likely to be of interest to the world at large, is a particularly suitable field for outside help. So are special investigations of development projects, or pilot schemes, since groups of scientists or technicians can come from outside and complete these within a reasonably short period. Foundations and scientific institutions in Britain, North America, or elsewhere, as well as international agencies, can be specially useful in providing both finance and personnel for research and technical investigations in the African Territories.

5 *Education in the broadest sense.* Educational aid is to be regarded as a form of pump-priming. Therefore, while the greatest need is likely to be qualified academic staff and teachers of various kinds, outside capital also can legitimately be invested in the establishment or expansion of colleges, training centers, and other educational institutions. Within the educational field the most appropriate subjects for aid are universities and higher colleges; technical colleges; agricultural institutes; other vocational training centers, including those for medical and public health staff; training centers for cooperative, community development and adult education workers; schemes for helping African traders both with credit and instruction; and schemes to help Africans gain higher qualifications or pursue specialist courses overseas. With these I would couple,

as equally appropriate for aid, programs for health education and in certain cases for the eradication of particular diseases, and rural development schemes designed to stimulate progress in the less advanced areas of a country, thus preventing lack of balance in development. Here again, in all these things, foundations and international agencies can usefully undertake aid projects, and professional societies, both national and international, have a valuable part to play in fostering contacts with the corresponding societies in the African countries for the discussion of technical and specialist problems.

6 *Overseas officials*. Until sufficient numbers of qualified local officials can be trained, the part which overseas officials have to play in administration, technical and scientific services, economic planning, and the training of local staff is of the greatest possible importance. Indeed the retention or replacement of these officials is perhaps the greatest practical problem of newly independent countries. Special arrangements by the Governments of these countries or guarantees as to the future of these men and women by the Government of the former administering power are both important and useful, but cannot completely solve the problem. Suggestions have been made that an international civil service should be set up for this purpose; to make such a service a fully effective instrument it would be necessary to give it a sufficiently long-term character to enable it to recruit and retain first class staff, to create a sense of continuity, and to build up a high esprit de corps. Another suggestion is that a Commonwealth civil service should be established to provide officers for whatever Commonwealth Government wished to employ them; this would involve a new departure in Commonwealth relations. I do not propose to discuss these questions in greater detail; although in my view they are crucial.

All this leads to the next question. Who is going to provide the outside aid which the African countries need and ask for? Britain under the Colonial Development and Welfare Act,

France under FIDES, and Belgium under the *Plan Decennal* have since the Second World War provided very large grants for economic and social development. The British Government has recently announced its intention of extending the Colonial Development and Welfare Act after 1960 so that grants to dependent countries in Africa and elsewhere can go on. The investment ceiling of the Colonial Development Corporation has also been raised to $420 million. Technical assistance will continue to be available to independent countries which want it.

But there are limits to the amount of overseas aid which Britain can provide in her present economic circumstances. Our ability to give aid depends on the strength of sterling and this would be threatened by over-committal of our resources. Apart from this, newly independent countries will not wish to go only to the old administering powers for assistance in capital and personnel. Through our past experience in these countries, our knowledge of their problems and our friendship with their people we are of course well qualified to provide them with assistance, and the independent countries themselves are likely to go on looking to us to a considerable extent. But I believe that they will look in increasing measure to the United States, as they are already doing. The United States has already given valuable help to the African Territories, both in capital and personnel. The need for both these is steadily growing, and in its new Development Loan Fund the United States has, I believe, provided an instrument which is particularly well suited to expand this form of aid from America to Africa. The problem seems to me to be so great, so important, and so urgent that it needs to be tackled by the Western world as a whole. The Technical Assistance Administration of the United Nations, the Specialized Agencies, and the International Bank can of course help very materially and should be made full use of.

But the main initiative must, I believe, come from the countries of the Western world.

What in fact is the Western world's interest in aiding Africa? I believe that we have three essential interests. The first is moral and humanitarian—to help the peoples of these African countries to carry forward the task of development undertaken by the administering powers during the last two generations. The second is our own economic interest—our need for raw materials from Africa and our wish to trade with these countries and supply them with the capital and consumer goods which they need in increasing measure. Finally, there is a political interest—to help them to remain stable and friendly to the Western world. The African countries themselves want to press on with development—indeed they are determined to do so. They want to trade with us and sell us their raw materials. They want to remain friendly to us, and have embraced Western ideas and ideals. In fact the interests of the Western world and of the African countries are broadly the same.

The need to give aid is often linked with the threat of communism. I do not regard the communist interest in the African countries as the main reason for our aiding them; most emphatically I would state that there are other perfectly good reasons for doing this. But the communist interest is something which we cannot leave out of account. This has been steadily increasing, although so far the communists have made only a limited impression on Africa south of the Sahara. The communists have some obvious advantages. The absence of racial bars in the Soviet Union is obviously attractive to Africans. Although the Soviet Union covers an enormous area including a variety of peoples, they have no overseas responsibilities and have therefore been able to pose as the chief critics of those who have. Increasingly also the Soviet Union will be in a position to supply aid to underdeveloped countries as their own industrial development goes forward.

We have some serious competition to face and there is no ground for complacency; but equally there is no reason for excessive alarm. Mr. George Kennan has pointed out that leading people in these countries are likely to be fully able to take the measure of Moscow's motives and methods. In our own policy in Africa, if we pursue it resolutely and recognize that the most vital thing in it is to work in cooperation with Africans, we have a perfectly good answer to the communist approach. The answer is inherent in all that I have tried to say. In territories which are still dependent we must maintain steady political advance accompanied by social and economic progress. To independent countries the Western world must give adequate help from outside in capital, personnel, and technical assistance so that they can keep up the momentum of their development programs, and this help must be given without military or political strings. If we give it and if their development goes forward smoothly, the conditions in which communism flourishes can be avoided. But I repeat again that the fear of communism is not to be regarded as the main reason why we give this help. We give it partly in our own interests, but largely, I believe, because of what Mr. Adlai Stevenson has described as our moral commitment to humanity.

This brings me to my final point. I believe it important that the United States and Britain should realize that our interests in Africa are broadly the same. We both want steady movement towards self-government. We both recognize that this requires stability, economic progress, and outside help. We both want to be friends with these countries and to do business with them. The similarity of our interests is I believe increasingly recognized by informed opinion on both sides of the Atlantic. But there are still numbers of less well informed people on both sides who do not see things in this way and continue with outmoded attitudes, suggesting differences between us which I believe do not really exist. There are still some people in

Britain, perhaps not very many, who look at Africa through paternalistic spectacles and regard the transfer of power to Colonial people as a form of defeat, instead of what it is, a fulfillment of our traditional policy and a strengthening of the Commonwealth and the free world. There are still quite a number of people in the United States who, in this cold world, find anti-colonialism a comfortable blanket to wrap themselves up in. I plead that these out-of-date appurtenances should be sloughed off. We have a cooperative job to do. To do it successfully we need to understand each other and the nature of the job.